Chosen

THE STORY OF GOD AND HIS PEOPLE

Daniel J. Simundson
and
David L. Tiede

Augsburg Publishing House
Minneapolis

Chosen

The Story of God and His People

Prepared under the auspices of
the Division for Life and Mission in the Congregation
and the Board of Publication
of the American Lutheran Church

This Student Book is accompanied by a Teacher's Guide

Theodore J. Vinger, editor

Graphic design by Koechel Design

Photos: Luoma, page 8. H. Armstrong Roberts, 20, 81a, 138.
Rohn Engh, 22, 28, 106. Wallowitch, 32, 49a, 89, 117, 143,
152, 184, 194. Ewing Galloway, 76, 199. Religious News Service,
81b, 110, 170. Hedgecoth, 93. Daniel D. Miller, 148.
Almasy of Three Lions, 154. Arland Erickson, 163.
Bob W. Smith, 173. Vivienne, 187. Richard T. Lee, 191.

Scripture quotations unless otherwise noted are from
Revised Standard Version of the Bible, copyright 1946-71 by
Division of Christian Education, National Council of Churches,
and are used by permission.

Manufactured in U.S.A.

Contents

Preface

It is our hope that this book will be helpful to those beginning a serious study of the Bible and to those who are interested in discovering how the many pieces of the biblical story fit together. Of course the only way to get the whole story is to read the Bible itself, and certainly our little volume could never claim to improve on the way the story is told there.

But this book attempts to provide an "interpretative survey" in which the biblical story is outlined in as close to chronological order as possible. Summaries are given of what was going on in history in order to provide an overview of the sweep of the action in the biblical period. Key texts are chosen to illustrate the major themes running throughout the Scriptures with continual reference to the central revelation of God's grace, his never-failing love.

This book should not be used in place of reading the Bible. The particular texts which are mentioned in each chapter provide the focus for the discussion. The chapter is merely an attempt to help the reader get into the biblical material by raising questions that arise from those passages and making connections between the story and our world. Thus the central objective is to get the reader started interpreting the Christian Scriptures rather than presuming to provide answers to all the difficult questions. This means that a good modern translation such as the Revised Standard Version or perhaps Today's English Version should be used rather than a paraphrase.

A Christian needs to know the Bible and to know enough about it to read it with openness, understanding, and enthusiasm. From generation to generation, the Holy Spirit has renewed, inspired, challenged, and comforted God's people through the Scriptures. It is our hope that this book will help prepare members of a new generation for a lifetime of that kind of study of the Scriptures. In that hope, we dedicate this book to Susan, Ann Marie, Peter, and Kathryn.

Daniel J. Simundson
David L. Tiede
January 1, 1976

The Story of God's Love Part 1

The gift of books

A wealthy man wanted to do something very special for his son's 18th birthday. He wanted to give him something that would be more than just another gift with an expensive price tag. Finally, he hit on an idea. He would give his son a whole shelf of books—books that had inspired him and helped him set standards for his own life.

There would be different kinds of books in this collection, some very old and others from more recent times. There would be books of history, poetry, short stories, wise sayings by famous people, biography, adventure, and a book of hymns and prayers. Some of the books would be serious, but others would be humorous.

At age 18, the son might not be too thrilled with such a gift. Yet as he thought about it the father became convinced that these books would be one of the finest gifts he could give his son. He knew that as the boy grew and learned more about life, he would come to realize this too.

The gift of the Bible

Our Bible is something like that shelf of books. Though it comes bound together in one volume, it is really a collection of many different books written over a long period of time. These books tell the story of God and his relationship with his people. The writers tell how they have seen God in their lives. What

9

they wrote has become the standard of belief for people like us who follow in later generations. So the story told in the books of the Bible is also our story.

Certain events stand out in the story that the Bible tells. In the Old Testament the most important event is probably the exodus, in which God responds to the suffering of his people by delivering them from slavery and guiding them to new life in a new land.

In the New Testament the most important events are in the life, death, and resurrection of Jesus. In a very special way they show us who God is and how much he loves us. These events are mentioned again and again throughout the books of the Bible as men and women proclaim their understanding of what it means to live in a right relationship with God.

But God's people look for a word from him in everything that takes place. It is not only in the spectacular, miraculous events that they see him at work. They believe in a God who is active in the world and cares about it. Therefore everything that happens has the possibility of being a message from God for people of faith.

So the Bible is not only concerned with the exodus and the resurrection. There are many other examples of God telling his people something they should hear. There is a message in the movement of an ancient wanderer named Abraham, or the birth of a long-awaited child like Isaac, or the coming of an illness or a sudden cure, or prosperity or drought.

Throughout the history of his people, God has sent poets, prophets, storytellers, priests, and historians to interpret what all these things mean in the life of the people. Those who were proved by later developments to be speaking a word from God were remembered. Their words have become the Bible.

Before going on to study individual parts of the Bible, let us make two general statements: (1) the Bible is both a divine and a human collection of writings, and (2) in spite of great differences among parts of the Bible, there is one main theme running through it from beginning to end.

The divine/human book

The Bible is a *divine book* because in it we find a word from God. It is the only record we have of his choosing a people

Nave's TOPICAL BIBLE

Keyes

Story of the BIBLE WORLD

Hans J. Hillerbrand

The Reformation

THE SLAVS in European History and Civilization

Church in History

G. CAMPBELL MORGAN

...ture of the United States

MOODY PRESS

to be his own. There is no other place to find out about events like the exodus from Egypt or the resurrection of Jesus.

The most important reason for studying the Bible is to learn more about God. We search through it for answers to our religious questions, and we identify ourselves with those ancient people who encountered God in their lives.

So every biblical passage should be looked at from a theological point of view—we should ask religious questions of it. We should think about it, pray about it, argue with it, compare it with other passages, and try to involve it in our own life. As we do this we should expect that God will speak a word to us.

It is important in this process to look at all of the Bible, the Old Testament as well as the New, the unfamiliar parts as well as those that sound familiar, the parts that make us squirm and feel uncomfortable as well as the parts that make us feel warm and comforted. Since God speaks to us through the words of Holy Scripture, perhaps he is saying something new and exciting to us in the difficult or less familiar parts of the Bible.

But the Bible is also a *human book*. God reveals himself in the lives of his people. Individual humans tell the story in their own language, influenced by their own personality, culture, and understanding.

Not all people understand God's activity in our world in exactly the same way. There is always a bit of mystery in what God is doing so that no human words or thoughts can sum it up perfectly. The human factor in the writing of the biblical books is a difficult thing to understand. But it is a very important thing to keep in mind as we begin to study in detail some specific Bible passages.

This concept will help us as we come across passages that give us difficulty. We have trouble, for example, with stories in which the "good" people in the Bible act terribly, killing people, committing adultery, lying, and stealing. Or stories that seem to disagree with what we learn about the world from science— like the story of creation and the record of many miracles. Or laws from the Bible that are continually quoted to keep people in their place—the role of women in the church, for example.

This divine book is also a human collection of books written at specific times in history by real people who were interpreting God's will in terms of what they understood about their world and themselves. So we recognize both the divine and human qualities in the Bible. But we also recognize that there is a central theme running through the Bible from beginning to end.

The unity of the book

The rich man who chose the books for his son did not confine his choice to one period of time or one kind of writing. Neither would he choose books that only presented one point of view on any subject. If his son was to know what life is about, he should have a rich variety of many different ideas, from different ages, and presented in different ways.

There is variety like that in the Bible. The Old Testament tells the story from the beginning of the world to the time just before Christ. It is especially concerned with the time from Abraham (about 1800 B.C.) to the time of Ezra and Nehemiah (about 400 B.C.). It was written over a period of about 1000 years and includes several different kinds of books. It is not simply history. There are also songs, psalms, proverbs, stories, parables, laws, and more.

In spite of all these different kinds of books and different times and different authors, there is a unifying theme which runs through the Bible. It is the theme of God's grace, his love which never gives up on people. It shows itself in the goodness of creation. The Bible shows how this love of God is continually pushed aside by humans who are disobedient and proud and will not trust in what God has promised them. Yet God continues to love.

There are many times in the biblical story when God could have thrown up his hands in disgust and said, "I've had it! I'm finished with trying to get through to these people." But he refused to do that. He kept coming back to try some new way to reach these people that he loved so much. We shall see this theme again and again as we look through the books of both the Old and the New Testament. It is the theme which holds all of these different biblical books together.

The Bible is the story of God and his people. It was written by his people in response to what God was doing in their lives. As part of God's people, we read the Bible to hear a word from God in our own day—a word that continues to call us to serve him and his world.

Promises, Promises

Introducing Abraham

People are on the move all the time. Few people spend their lives in the same location. Some may move only across the field or around the block, while others move back and forth across the country and even around the world.

There is such movement in our past also. Our fathers, grandfathers, or great-grandfathers left familiar places, a language they could understand, friends and relatives, and set out for a strange new place.

Why do people move? It is usually a difficult experience, and yet it happens all the time. People move because they think life will be better in a new place. Maybe the old place was unpleasant, or maybe it wasn't so bad, but the new place appears more attractive. Regardless, moving is always a bit of a gamble. We move in the hope that it will be better for us in that unknown new place.

Almost 4000 years ago, a man named Abraham picked up and left the country where he had grown up. Many people of that day had made similar moves. But when Abraham moved, it was the beginning of God's people, the people we read about in the Bible, the family of God that we also belong to.

The story of Abraham's decision to leave one place and go to another becomes the story of how God chose a people to be his own. God made an agreement with Abraham. God told him that he would do great things for him and his children and that the whole world would be better off because of him. Abraham was to trust God and believe that the promises would come true. All Abraham had was that promise from God, but for him that was enough. And he left upper Mesopotamia (now a part of Iraq) and moved to what we know as Palestine, or the state of Israel.

This is not just ancient history. The relationship that Abraham had with God is like the one that we still have with God. We are part of the family. God continues to promise to be with us and guide us. He tells us, as he told Abraham, that he is our God and we are his people, and there is nothing that will ever cause him to break that promise. The only thing he asks of us is to believe that promise, as Abraham did.

It is not always easy to do that. Sometimes our lives get confused and messed up. Sometimes we are disappointed and hurt. At times it would be easy to give up and begin to doubt that God cares. We all remember praying hard for something and not getting it.

Abraham's story is like that, too. What is special about Abraham is that he continued to trust in God's promises even though there were many times when obstacles were thrown in his way, and it looked as if God had been deceiving him and leading him on a wild goose chase. But Abraham hung in there, and God's promises were kept. That is the story of the Bible. And it is also our story.

The story of Abraham is told in the book of Genesis, Chapters 12 to 24. These stories tell of God's love and Abraham's response to that love in spite of many difficulties. We shall look at a few samples of that story.

An amazing agreement
Genesis 12:1-3; 15:1-6

In these passages we read how it all started. These are two versions of the covenant that God made with Abraham and they show us much about both God and Abraham. There are two words that we should learn as we look at these stories: *covenant* and *faith*. A covenant is like an agreement, or a legal contract, or a treaty. Two people or two businesses or two countries get together and make an agreement. Both parties in the covenant agree to do certain things. That is, they make promises to each other as to what they will do.

For example, a girl makes an agreement with her mother that if she practices her piano lesson every day for the next five days, she will be allowed to spend the weekend at her friend's cabin. Or a homeowner agrees to sell his home to Mr. Smith, if Smith agrees to pay him $40,000. Or Russia makes a treaty with the United States that it will remove its missiles from a certain country if the U.S. will also remove some missiles.

In Genesis 12 God made an agreement with Abraham. He promised that Abraham would be the father of a great nation, that he would be blessed and that all nations would be blessed through him and his descendants. The strange thing is that God made all these promises without asking for anything in return.

Ordinarily in a covenant, *both* parties have to agree to something. But with God, no strings are attached. No ifs, ands, or buts. God had already decided about Abraham. Once God makes such a decision, there is no changing it. Even if Abraham and his descendants in later generations should turn away and become disobedient, God will stick by his promises. What an amazing thing for God to do!

An amazing response

Abraham's response is also amazing. This is where the other key word must be mentioned: *faith*. Abraham's reaction to this offer by God was to believe. That is, he trusted God, he believed the promises, he left his native country with the confidence and assurance that God really meant what he said. That is faith.

Having such faith may sound simple, but it is not. The natural reaction to an offer like that given by God would be to get suspicious. Abraham could have thought to himself, "What does God really want? What is he after? He tells me he loves me and is going to do all this for me, but it sounds too good to be true. It's hard to believe it when someone promises you great things without expecting something in return. There must be a catch."

In every human life things happen that cause us to wonder if God really is keeping his promises. Abraham's life was no exception. In fact, the biblical stories about him are mainly concerned with the things that seemed to stand in the way and block the fulfillment of those promises. It was as if God's promises and Abraham's faith were constantly being put to the test.

The problem was that Abraham did not have a son. There was no way that Abraham could ever be the father of a mighty nation with descendants as numerous as the stars in heaven if he did not have a son. With no children, God's promise seemed like a cruel joke, a raising of false hopes, an impossible thing to believe. But Abraham trusted God.

Three challenges
Genesis 12:10-20; 18:9-15

The first big challenge to God's promise comes very early in the story and it consisted of two threats. One was the famine. If Abraham and his wife starved to death, that would be the end of what God promised Abraham. The land of Canaan, where Abraham had moved at God's command, was a very dry place; some years there were no crops because of the drought. When such things happened, the people would go down to Egypt, where there was usually plenty of food because of the water from the Nile River.

The second threat arose because of the beauty of Sarah, Abraham's wife. Abraham was afraid he would be killed so the king of Egypt could make Sarah his wife. To keep that from happening, Abraham had her pretend that she was his sister. That saved his life, but it meant she ended up in the Pharaoh's harem instead of in Abraham's tent.

This is a story that the descendants of Abraham probably

enjoyed telling. It shows that even the great man of faith, Abraham, sometimes did things that we consider wrong—in this case, he was so worried about his own life and safety that he was willing to give up his wife to another man. Remember, God did not choose Abraham because of anything that he had done to deserve such special attention. God's love and his promise to Abraham were simply gifts, given to an imperfect human being who behaved like us in many ways.

The age of Abraham and Sarah was the second challenge to God's promise. Abraham and Sarah had come to this new land. They had believed God. But even for these people there

were moments when they must have had their doubts. Abraham was by then 100 years old and Sarah was 90. Everyone knows that people that old can't have babies.

One day three visitors came to see Abraham. They were bringing a message from the Lord that by the next spring Sarah would have a son. Sarah overheard the message and laughed to herself because she knew that it was impossible. Her laughter was a temporary weakening of faith, and she was questioned

about it: "Is anything too hard for the Lord?" But finally God's promise was kept: Sarah had a child (Gen. 21:1-3).

But then came the hardest test of all. It is one of the strangest and most interesting stories in the Bible.

The hardest challenge
Genesis 22:1-14

God had finally blessed Abraham with a son, Isaac. Abraham's faith had been shown to be correct. But now God wanted him to do something which didn't make any sense. After waiting all these years for a son, now he was supposed to go up on a mountain and kill that son as a sacrifice to God.

We don't know what Abraham thought. The story tells us that when God told him to do this, he went to do it. Whether he doubted God's word or had some thoughts of defying God and saying, "I won't do it," we just don't know. All we know from the story is that Abraham was again faithful. He trusted God and obeyed him.

This is a strange story. The whole idea of sacrificing an animal or a human being for the greater good of other people is something that is hard for us to understand. We tend to think of such ideas as barbaric, and yet Christians often talk about how Jesus was a sacrifice for our sin. We shall have to think more about that later in this book.

In this particular case, God did not actually demand the life of Isaac. He stopped Abraham in time. But why did he make Abraham and Isaac go through all this? That question is hard for us to answer. Perhaps it was to teach that God does not demand human sacrifices as some other ancient religions did. As the story appears in our Bibles, it is most important as another in a series of stories that shows the faith of Abraham and the promise of God that will not fail even in the most serious situation. Abraham dared to trust God even when things made no sense to him at all, and God did not fail him.

So Abraham, the spiritual father of all Jews and Christians, did leave a son, who had sons. They had sons and the world was blessed through them, especially through that son, born in Bethlehem many generations later, who was named Jesus.

In the Beginning

What came before Abraham?
Genesis 1 and 2

It is not enough to begin the story with Abraham. We have to go back further. We want to know what happened before that. We want to know how the world began. The people who wrote the Bible had the same kind of questions we do. So they went back to the very beginning. They told stories about the creation of the earth, the sun, moon, stars, dry land, plants, animals, and, most significant of all, men and women.

There are three important things to remember when studying the creation story. The first is that the God of the Hebrews created everything. The second is that the creation is good. The third is that God gave this creation as a gift to all human beings and told them to use it properly. If we can keep these points clearly in mind, then we have understood the religious message of Genesis 1 and 2.

The creation story is a religious answer to the kinds of questions people ask. It is not meant to be a scientific account of how the universe began. There are all kinds of scientific theories about that, and some of them are in violent disagreement with others.

Neither is the biblical story meant to be a scientific explanation of the order in which certain kinds of life appeared. There are also many theories about that—theories that explain how one kind of living creature could evolve from another kind of creature.

The biblical story of creation is not an eyewitness account by a newspaper reporter who was watching everything happen and writing it down. There could hardly have been any human eyewitness during the first five days since human beings weren't even created until the sixth day.

When people try to make the biblical account fit in with all the things we learn in school about astronomy, geology, biology, and evolution, they run into problems. One of the biggest problems is to think of the world being created in six days when there is all kinds of evidence that it has taken millions of years. Some have tried to solve this problem by saying that a "day" in the Bible could be a way of talking about thousands or even millions of years. In 2 Peter 3:8, we read, "But do not ignore this one fact, beloved, that with the Lord one day is as a thousand years, and a thousand years as one day." Other people have chosen to argue that the Bible must be "scientifically accurate," and therefore all the findings of modern science must be questioned.

Remember what was said in the first chapter of the book? The Bible is both a divine and a human book. It is God's Word to us, but written by human beings in words that others can understand. The writer talks about the world in terms that were known to him. You would not expect someone writing 3000 years ago to have the same kind of understanding of the universe as someone living after the discoveries of men like Galileo, Darwin, Einstein, and those men who have traveled to the moon and back.

However we solve these kinds of questions for ourselves, we should remember that the Bible is primarily concerned with religious questions—questions about who God is and what he thinks about us. And the way it answers those questions is what makes it the Word of God for us. The creation stories in Genesis 1 and 2 are answers to questions like these: Who is responsible for the creation? Is the world and all of creation a good thing? What are we human beings supposed to do with it?

Who is responsible?

Who is responsible for this world? Who made it? Was it by accident? Is some god responsible? If so, which god? The Hebrew storyteller answered this question by saying that the same God who called Abraham and made promises to him is the one who created heaven and earth and all that is in them.

That is a very important thing to say. Abraham's God is not just one god among many. He is *the* God. He is not just a tribal god who for some reason liked Abraham and promised to watch out for him. He is not in competition with other gods from other nations where people also happen to believe that they have a god who is watching out for them. Abraham's God is the only God there is. He is the God of all people.

God had a mission for Abraham. He loves all the world and used Abraham and his children to carry the message of his faithfulness and love so that all the world would know about the one true God. Through Abraham, all the families of the earth would be blessed.

The God of Abraham made the world. It was not by accident. It was by design. And the God of Abraham loves all that he has made.

Is it good?

Is the world and all of creation a good thing? On a lovely spring day, with blue sky and green grass and a family that loves us, it is easy to believe that the creation is good.

But when disaster strikes, when the rains don't come and thousands of people in Africa are starving, when an earthquake destroys a whole city, when a blizzard kills dozens of people and thousands of animals, when tornadoes sweep across the plains, when a young mother dies of cancer, when someone whom we want to love us seems to hate us, when nations continue to drop bombs on each other, then we are not so certain that this is the greatest of all worlds. Who is responsible? Couldn't the world have been made just a little better? Why did God make mosquitoes or the virus that causes the common cold?

Some religions have looked at the bad things going on in the world and decided that the creation is not a good thing. In the time when our biblical creation story was written, some religions taught that the world was made from the body of an evil goddess. Certain eastern religions say that a human being finds salvation by somehow escaping from the world. Even Christianity sometimes sounds like this, telling us that the things of the flesh are not as good as the things of the Spirit and warning us to be wary of the dangers of this world.

So there are different ways of looking at the evil things in the world. But the creation story makes it clear that the God who made everything meant it for good. In Genesis 1, we are told that after God made something he looked at it and saw that it was good. This happened six times and then verse 31 sums it up: "And God saw everything that he had made, and behold, it was very good." God is good, and what he made was good. If there is something wrong with the world as we know it, it is not because God did not make it to be good.

What do we do with it?
Genesis 1:26-31

What are we supposed to do with this world that God has made? What is our responsibility as human beings? Are we just one of the many creatures that God has made or are we something special? What does God expect from us?

God created us in his own image. No other creature is so described. Human beings are different from everything else that God has made. They are in his image and they are to have dominion (power, control, authority) over everything else that God has made.

What does it mean to be made in God's image? Does it mean we look like God, or think like God, or have a special ability to have a relationship with God? Students of the Bible have wondered about the meaning of these words ever since they were first written.

Whatever else it means, at least this is sure: human beings are different from every other creature on the face of the earth. They can relate to God in a way that no plant or animal can. They can communicate with him, and he with them. And with this special status comes special responsibility.

Human beings are to have dominion over the world, which means that we are to use and enjoy the creation for good purposes. We are to take care of this world and see that everything is run properly. This reminds us of three subjects that are being discussed today: ecology, over-population, and the importance of women.

Ecology is a study of the relationship between living things and their environment. There is concern that we are using up too many of our natural resources. If human beings destroy the landscape, they might ruin the beauty of the earth, or even bring on disasters like flooding. If we pollute the water, we don't have enough to drink, or we cause diseases, or we kill the fish. If we use chemicals to destroy the bugs, then we kill the birds. If there is no more land for the wild animals to live in, soon they will begin to disappear. Human beings have dominion over the earth. We have the power to keep the world a good place—or we can destroy it. This is a great responsibility.

A similar problem is the one of overpopulation. When the world was created, there was a need for humans to be fruitful and multiply and fill up the world (Gen. 1:28). Now there are so many people in the world that there may not be enough room for them to live or enough food for them to eat. The command which God gave to be fruitful may not be our biggest concern anymore. Now we need to use our dominion to see that there are not too many people for the world to support.

The creation story tells about the creation of men and women. Some people have argued from Gen. 2:20-23 that women are not on the same level as men. They say that since man was created first, he is more important. The woman, they say, was only created later in order to be a helper and companion for him.

We must be very careful that we do not use biblical passages to support our own particular prejudices. In this case, it is a good idea to compare Gen. 2:20-23 with Gen. 1:27. In the latter passage, there is no distinction made between men and women. God created both in his own image.

Many students of the Bible think that we have two creation stories here—one ending in the middle of Gen. 2:4 and the other beginning with the second part of the verse. There are some significant differences, one of which is the way in which the creation of woman is described.

So the creation stories go back before Abraham to answer some further questions that we all wonder about. The answers are not scientific explanations of how the world was created, but answers to our questions about God and his world. The God of Abraham made the world. It is good. And we humans have a special responsibility to take care of it.

There is still a nagging problem. What went wrong? How do we explain those bad things that sometimes happen to us and others? We certainly don't live in the Garden of Eden anymore. Something really went wrong. That is the subject of our next chapter.

Trouble in the Garden

The good old days

The Garden of Eden must have been a great place. No problems, diseases, wars, or crowded cities. Everyone had just what was needed. All you had to do if you wanted food was to go out and pick something off a tree. No one was afraid of death because it didn't exist. No one had a guilty conscience, for there was no sin.

The people who wrote this story looked back longingly at those good old days. But those days did not last. The sons of Abraham who told this story knew that the world wasn't like that anymore. What had happened? What happened to the Garden of Eden? What happened to God's good world?

Genesis 1 and 2 tell us that the God of Abraham made our world. It is a good place, and we humans have the responsibility of taking care of it. Genesis 3 tells us what went wrong. Chapters 4 through 11 of Genesis go on to give more examples of how bad things became. By the end of Genesis 11 it looks very hopeless.

Like the creation stories, the stories in Genesis 3 to 11 are not meant to be scientific history. There is no way we can check the details to make sure everything happened exactly as described in Genesis. These stories are meant to be answers to the religious questions of those who told the stories and those who heard them. Since we are part of that same family of storytellers, these stories become answers to our questions too.

The most important questions in these stories are these:

(1) Whose fault is it that the world got so messed up, and (2) How is God going to help us out of this miserable situation? The answers to these questions are (1) It is not God's fault, but ours, and (2) God loves us and has provided help.

Who caused the trouble?

Genesis 3:1—11:9

Who is responsible for the evil in our world? Is it God? After all, he made everything. If he wanted it to be good, didn't he have enough power to make it stay good? Perhaps he should have done some things a little differently.

For one thing, he made some demands on his people. He told them not to eat the fruit of a certain tree. Nothing looks quite so attractive as something we are told we cannot have. We may never think of "walking on the grass" or "cheating in the test" or "reading that nasty book" until someone tells us not to do it. Maybe God made a mistake in leaving one tempting tree in the middle of the garden and then telling Adam and Eve not to eat from it. What did he expect them to do?

Another thing God did was to allow Adam and Eve to have the freedom of choice. He could have made people into robots so that they would always do only what he told them to do. If he had done that, then no evil would have come into the world. As long as there is the possibility of choice, we can disobey and cause trouble.

And another thing. If God made everything, why did he make the snake? Maybe everything would have been all right if there had been no snake to put ideas into the woman's head. Maybe God should have done something about that.

God has some responsibility here. It is his world. But the coming of evil is not his fault. He expected people to trust and obey him, but he allowed them to be free so he could have a relationship of trust and love with them. We cannot fault God for letting human beings be really human. The fault lies elsewhere.

What about the snake? Who was that snake anyway? He was more clever than any wild creature that God made. He talked, and he tried to get the man and woman into trouble. Where did he come from? The Bible has no word of explanation about this. He suddenly appears in the story. That's all we know.

In this story the snake is not called "Satan" or "the devil." He is referred to only as "the serpent." We have come to think of this creature as being the devil. But even if we think of it as the devil, this still doesn't help too much. Where did the devil come from? Why would God allow such a creature in his good world?

The mysterious presence of the snake in this story reminds us that we don't know enough to give a complete answer to the question of whose fault it is that the world turned bad. The snake is partly at fault, but we don't know who he is or where he came from.

The only other characters in the story are the man and the woman. What is their responsibility in all this? As you read the story, it says that things went wrong after the man and woman disobeyed God and ate from the forbidden tree. If we are trying to place the blame, it looks as if the best candidates are the human beings who did not do as they were told.

Some people have decided that the woman is more to blame than the man. The woman was the first to be tempted. She ate and gave to her husband. This is a passage sometimes quoted by those who want to argue that women are not equal to men. It is a poor use of the passage. The man and the woman were in it together. They were equally guilty. See how quick the man was to excuse himself and to blame "the woman whom thou gavest to be with me" (Gen. 3:12).

The man tried to squirm out of his own responsibility and blame both the woman and God. That is a very common thing for us to do when we are caught doing wrong. We refuse to accept our own responsibility and look for someone else to blame.

Disobedience on the part of the man and woman spoiled the Garden of Eden. Maybe it's not such a big deal just to eat some fruit that you were told to keep away from. But this act showed a basic unwillingness to trust God and to believe that he knows what is best. It showed a desire to want to be independent of God. Such doubt causes a break in the good relationship between God and us.

So, the coming of evil into our world is a very difficult thing to understand. There are no easy answers. No matter how we try, there are things about it we cannot explain. The Bible deals

with this question of evil by telling this story. God made a good world, though he allowed for human freedom and that meant the possibility of trouble. The snake made it easier for them to do wrong. He egged them on and encouraged their disobedience. But the man and woman could not blame him. It was their own responsibility. Evil entered the world because they disobeyed God.

Now people were ashamed because they were naked. The snake was doomed to crawl on his belly in the dust, and a never-ending hostility arose between the snake and human beings. There would be pain in childbirth, and people would have to work hard to make a living. Human beings would die and return to the dust from which they came. Once evil came into the world, there was no stopping it. There is the suggestion in God's statement, however, that he will see to it that evil is eventually crushed.

The story continues with three more examples of how bad things became. First, Cain killed his brother, and jealousy and murder were loose in the world. Later, God became so disgusted with the human race that he considered destroying the whole creation. He found Noah and his family the only ones worth saving.

Finally, in a great show of arrogance and pride, some people tried to build a tower up to the sky and become like God. In order to prevent this, God confused their language so that they found it impossible to communicate with each other. In time, the good life that was possible in the Garden of Eden became only a distant memory.

Who has the answer?

The answer to our second question is that God still cares. He has not given up. After each of the disasters in Genesis 3–11, there is a small glimmer of hope—an example of God reaching out to do something for us.

After the catastrophe of Genesis 3, we read this strange verse (3:21): "And the Lord God made for Adam and for his wife garments of skins, and clothed them." In a beautiful way, this little verse says something about God, who keeps coming after us, stooping down to where we are, concerned about our ordinary human needs, doing whatever he can to help us make our life a little better and to show us how much he loves us.

After Cain killed Abel, he was punished by being sent away to wander in strange places among hostile people. But God did not leave Cain without protection. Gen. 4:14-15 tells how God put a mark on Cain so that people who might be tempted to slay him would know that he was under the Lord's protection.

After the flood, God assured Noah that such a disastrous thing would never happen again. As a sign of this promise, he set a rainbow in the sky, so that all who saw it would remember God's promise never again to abandon his people to total destruction. We are still reminded of God's promise to Noah when we see this beautiful sight.

We have already talked about God's promise to Abraham that first appears in Chapter 12 of Genesis. This promise was the response of God to the picture of despair and hopelessness given in Chapter 11. He accepted Abraham as he was, promised him great things, and made plans to use him and his sons to reach out to all of humanity with a message of hope and assurance.

That was the way the children of Abraham understood their world, and what went wrong, and what their own mission was to this world. They told these stories to their children because they wanted them to know and accept them as the answers to their religious questions. We, in our day, look to the same stories for the same reasons.

Tracing the Promise

Three generations

All of us love to hear stories about how it was back in the old days. That is the kind of history we have in the book of Genesis—stories about our ancestors. Remember how God gave a promise to Abraham that all the world would be blessed through him? Did God keep this promise?

The book of Genesis carries the story three generations beyond Abraham. We shall look briefly at what happens in each of those generations. Then we shall raise three religious questions that come to mind when we read these accounts of the sons of Abraham.

The first generation

Genesis 16; 21:8-21

Abraham had two sons. Isaac was the son of Abraham and Sarah. He was the long-hoped-for son through whom God would carry out his promises. He was the one whom God asked Abraham to sacrifice in that most difficult test of faith.

But Isaac was not Abraham's only son. Earlier, when it appeared that Sarah was never going to have a child, she agreed to let Abraham take her maid, Hagar, for a wife, so that she might bear a child for him. (There was no limit as to how many wives a man could have.) Abraham did this and Hagar had a child whose name was Ishmael. Hagar was an Egyptian and her son became the father of many nomadic Arabs.

Once Sarah gave birth to Isaac, however, it became clear that he would be the favored son rather than Ishmael. Ishmael's mother was a slave woman. Therefore, it was understood that the promise of God to bless all the world would be passed on through Isaac, not Ishmael. Ishmael and his mother were forced to leave and head south into the desert. But God continued to provide for them and promised to make a great nation of Ishmael, too.

In this first generation after Abraham, we have the story of the origin of the Arabs and an explanation of how Jews and Arabs are related and yet enemies.

The second generation
Genesis 25:19-28; 27:1-45

So our biblical story is concerned with Isaac, not Ishmael. Isaac had twin sons, Esau and Jacob. Esau was born first. Usually the older son was the favored one, the one who got the inheritance. But in Gen. 25:23, Rebekah was told that her younger son, Jacob, who would live in tents instead of out in the field and would be his mother's favorite, would be the stronger one.

Jacob and Esau represent two nations. Jacob's name was later changed to Israel (Gen. 32:22-32). Esau became the nation of Edom, a small kingdom southeast of Israel which was dominated by Israel off and on for several hundred years. This story explains the origin of these two nations, their close relationship, and why they were often enemies.

Up to this point, there has been a narrowing down. God was choosing a people who would bear his message and by whom the world would be brought back to him. He chose Abraham. Then he chose Isaac rather than Ishmael. And then Jacob rather than Esau. Jacob is the father of all the Israelites.

The third generation
Genesis 30:1-24

Jacob had 12 sons whose descendants became the 12 tribes of Israel. In those ancient days, before they had a king, the people of Israel were organized into tribes. All the tribes were related to each other because they all had the same ancestor, Jacob, who was also called Israel.

Joseph is sold to traders

But they certainly did not all have the same mother. There were four mothers. Rachel and Leah were sisters. Bilhah and Zilpah were the maids of Rachel and Leah. Since Rachel was the favorite wife, her children, Joseph and Benjamin, were special. The sons who were born to the servants had less status.

We learn much about the relative importance of the 12 tribes by knowing which mother they were descended from. Remember that Joseph was his father's favorite because he was the son of his favorite wife.

This is how the 12 tribes of Israel began. By the time Israel became a nation with a king, the tribes were not as important as they were at first. But they were still important in the minds of the people as they looked ahead to the fulfillment of God's promise in the future. It was not by accident that when Jesus was choosing followers, he chose 12 disciples, the number of the tribes of Israel.

Chapters 37 to 50 of Genesis concentrate on the story of one of Jacob's sons, Joseph. Through his story, we find the nation of Israel in Egypt instead of in the promised land. They survived the famine; God kept his promises. But there seems to have been a temporary sidetrack since they were no longer living in the land which God promised them. But God planned to send Moses to lead them back to the promised land. Before we go on to the story of Moses, however, we should look at three important religious questions.

The problem of being real people
Genesis 27:18-40

The first question we have to answer is how God could choose us and love us. When we read about these spiritual ancestors of ours we are reminded again and again that we are not chosen by God to be part of his family because we have done anything to deserve it. God has chosen us, as he chose these people, because he loves us *in spite of* who we are, not *because of* who we are.

The stories in Genesis are not about perfect people. They are not "good example" stories that we are supposed to look at and copy in our own lives. Oftentimes people are bothered when they read about how some of these people acted toward each other. For example, Sarah was cruel to Hagar when Hagar was able to give Abraham a son and she could not. When Sarah finally had a son of her own, she wanted to get rid of Hagar and Ishmael.

In a similar way, in Genesis 30 we saw the petty jealousy and self-concern shown among the wives of Jacob. And Jacob is a problem. The father of all the tribes of Israel resorted to trickery in order to get the birthright and blessing from his father by pretending to be Esau. His mother, Rebekah, was in on the trickery.

The Bible is not the story of perfect people who are always obedient to God and act in love toward one another. It is about real people who sometimes do very nasty things. It is about people we can understand because we know we are not perfect either. What is important is not that they were good people all the time. What is important is that God loved them and continued his relationship with them in spite of everything. He did not break off his promises because his people sometimes disappointed him.

The problem of playing favorites

The second question we have to deal with comes up again and again in these stories. Each time God picked one person to carry on his promise, that meant someone else was being excluded. If Isaac was picked, then Ishmael was not. If God chose Jacob, then Esau was left out in the cold. Is this fair? Should God do that?

We have just said that God doesn't choose us because we deserve it. Jacob was certainly no more deserving than Esau. Maybe even less so. And yet God picked Jacob. It is nice for us to believe that God has chosen us to be his people. But why does he have to cut off somebody else who is outside that family? Why should the ancient Hebrews get a special deal from God? Why should God favor Christians and not all the other people in the world?

There is no easy answer to this problem. But perhaps this will help. It is important to remember that God loves all that he has made. He is the creator of all people. But he needs someone to carry the message of his love. In every age he calls

Joseph and his brothers are reunited

some people to be obedient to him and make the sacrifice necessary to reach out to all human beings everywhere. We who are in the line of Abraham, Isaac, Jacob, and Jesus are not being chosen to get a special deal, wealth, fame, a long life, or any such rewards. We are called by God for a mission, for responsibility. It may be harder for us, not easier, because God has chosen us.

This is the kind of thing we have to remind ourselves of constantly. We are called to serve, not to relax and thank God that we are better off than other people.

The problem of evil

Genesis 50:15-21

The third question we have to deal with is the place of evil in God's plan. At the end of the Joseph story, we have another effort to explain the presence of evil in the world. Anyone can see that there was evil, pain, hostility, death, and other unpleasant things in the stories of Abraham and his sons. In Gen. 50:19-20, Joseph said to his brothers, "Fear not, for am I in the place of God? As for you, you meant evil against me; but God meant it for good, to bring it about that many people should be kept alive, as they are today."

Joseph's brothers were afraid he would get even with them for selling him into slavery. But he surprised them by forgiving them. He did not pretend that what they did was not evil. They were wrong. But God was able to use that evil for good. If Joseph had not been in Egypt, no preparation for the famine would have taken place and people would have died.

So even when we do bad things for bad reasons, God can make good come from them. We have to remember that God is in charge no matter what people do to each other.

Genesis ends with the people of Israel in Egypt. Already God's promise had been partially fulfilled because many people were blessed through the faith, courage, and insight of one of Abraham's descendants—Joseph. Things looked good for the sons of Jacob in Egypt. But they would soon change. God would still be with them, however, as times turned bad. It was almost time for Moses, the greatest Old Testament character of them all.

The Great Escape

Setting the stage

One of the saddest verses in the Bible is Exod. 1:8: "Now there arose a new king over Egypt, who did not know Joseph." Joseph—who had saved so many people by his wisdom and courage. Joseph—who had graciously forgiven his brothers and allowed them to live in Egypt. How could anyone forget Joseph?

We don't know who that new king was or how much time had passed. He apparently had his reasons for wanting his people to hate the Hebrews. Perhaps it was to give them someone to blame for all their troubles. Leaders have often done that in order to distract attention from their own failures. Or maybe the king's motive was just to get cheap labor. You can't build huge stone cities and monuments if you have to pay everyone a living wage. There certainly wouldn't be enough volunteers for the job.

So the king of Egypt dealt harshly with the Israelites. His attitude was: "Forget the good things the Hebrews have done. Think of them as an enemy in our midst who might try to rebel. Keep them under control. Put them to work building cities. Keep them so tired and beaten that they could never cause any trouble. If it looks as if too many of them are being born, kill off their boy babies."

The first chapter of Exodus gives us this kind of background information and sets the stage for the birth of Moses, the great leader whom God would use to free his people from slavery. The book of Exodus tells how God accomplished this great act of deliverance—an act so important to the people who wrote the Bible that they referred to it again and again.

Before we look at the story of Moses and the escape from Egypt in some detail, let us look at three truths which this story tells us about God.

First, God keeps his promises. He made promises to Abraham, Jacob, and Moses, and he stood by them. We can rely on him to keep his word. He continues to respond to our needs and to come to us even though we don't deserve it.

Second, God has compassion on those who are weak and oppressed. He takes pity on them, and responds by doing something. All through the Bible, God is on the side of those who need him the most, those who are hurting, those who are being mistreated by other people. God wants people to be free and happy and to live at peace with each other.

Third, God will send a deliverer when his people need one. Just when things seem to be hopeless, God sends someone to help. The greatest deliverer in the Old Testament was Moses. He became a model for future deliverers. When God finally sent Jesus Christ to save people from another kind of slavery, the gospel writers compared him to Moses. For example, Jesus, like Moses, barely escaped death from an evil king who killed all the boy babies in Bethlehem. Jesus fled to Egypt for safety, and then came out of Egypt, just as the Israelites did under Moses.

To tell the story of the deliverance from Egypt is to tell the story of Moses. There were three distinct periods in his life. Each was 40 years in length. The first 40 years he lived as an Egyptian. The next 40 years he lived as a sheepherder in the wilderness east of Egypt. The last 40 years he was a liberator, a leader of his people in the wilderness, and a lawgiver. The third period was the most important.

The first 40 years: Egypt
Exodus 2:1-15

The story of Moses in the bulrushes is one of the best-known stories in the Bible. Moses was born to a Hebrew family, but his life was in danger because of the king's order that all Hebrew boy babies should be killed. His mother put him in a basket in the weeds along the river. He was found there by the Pharaoh's daughter, who took him and raised him as her son.

We know nothing else about his youth. We might wonder if he knew that he was a Hebrew. Did his real mother, who nursed him for a time, tell him of his Hebrew ancestry? Did she tell him stories about Abraham, Jacob, and Joseph? Did his foster mother ever tell him where and how she found him? Did he go to school with other Egyptian children? It would be nice to know more about his youth.

When Moses was grown he saw an Egyptian mistreating a Hebrew slave. He killed the Egyptian and had to flee the country. Did he act out of human compassion, or did he know he was a Hebrew and feel he must defend one of his own people?

The second 40 years: Wilderness
Exodus 2:16—3:20

This period in Moses' life was very different from the previous one. If he was raised as the son of an Egyptian princess, he must have been accustomed to a very comfortable, even luxurious, life. Because of his act against the cruel Egyptian taskmaster, he was forced to give all that up and flee to the wilderness. It was a time of solitude and loneliness. One is reminded of how Jesus went off into the desert for 40 days to be tempted by the devil before he began his ministry.

In Exod. 2:16-17, there is another story about how Moses stepped in to help some people who were being mistreated. In this case it was the seven daughters of the priest of Midian who were being driven away from the well by some other shepherds. There was something in the character of Moses that caused him to act when he saw injustice being done. He and God were on the same wavelength in their compassion for people. (Note God's reactions to his people's troubles in Exod. 2:23-25 and 3:7-10.) It was not by accident that God picked Moses as the one to deliver his people.

Moses settled down, married one of the daughters of the priest of Midian, and seemed to be content with his new life.

You might think that would be the end of the story. He had made a new life for himself. He should be content now to slip quietly into middle age and then old age, working for his father-in-law, tending his sheep. But then a strange thing happened.

God appeared to Moses in a burning bush. That is, there was a fire in the bush, but the bush didn't burn up. Moses realized that he was in the presence of God, and it frightened him. God was actually talking to Moses and Moses was answering him. Most of us don't have experiences like this. We talk to God in prayers, but it is rare that we have the feeling that God is right there talking back to us.

In Bible stories, God often appears surrounded by fire. The fire serves two purposes: it lights the darkness and shows his presence, but it also is so bright that you cannot look directly into it. Because it shows that he is there and at the same time keeps people from seeing too much, fire is a very useful symbol of God's presence. The Old Testament states that it is more than one can bear to look at God face to face.

From the burning bush God said to Moses, "I have been so moved by the suffering of my people that I want to do something to free them. And you are my man. I want you to go to bring the people of Israel out of Egypt."

That sounded ridiculous to Moses. How could he convince the great Pharaoh to let the people go? Moses had many reasons why God ought to find somebody else for this job. "The Israelites won't believe me. They'll think I'm crazy. How can I prove to them that you called me to do this? Besides, I'm a terrible speaker. I'd have a hard time getting the words out. I could never persuade anybody to do anything. No, I'm sorry, God. You'd better get somebody else."

Moses had good reason to try to get out of this business. It would be tough for anyone to talk the mighty king of Egypt into giving up his cheap labor. It would be especially dangerous for Moses since he had fled Egypt as an outlaw. Maybe someone would remember him and throw him in jail or put him to death. That surely wouldn't accomplish what God had in mind. So Moses gave one excuse after another.

But none of the excuses was good enough. God had decided that this was his man. Moses was finally convinced, and headed back to Egypt. The second period of his life was ended. Any thought of a comfortable old age was gone. There were things he must do.

The third 40 years: Liberation
Exodus 12:21-42; 14:1-30

Moses was right. Pharaoh was a tough and stubborn man. With God's help, Moses tried one thing after another to convince the king of Egypt that he should let the Hebrews go. In Exodus 7–12, we read about a whole series of signs, wonders, and plagues that befell the Egyptians. But Pharaoh refused to budge. After foul water, frogs, gnats, flies, dead cattle, boils, hail, locusts, and a few other horrors, the Hebrews were still slaves in Egypt.

Perhaps Pharaoh just thought he was having a string of bad luck. You could probably explain away all these calamities. The Egyptians had been bothered with some of these problems before and they'd never had anyone telling them that God was doing this to them in order to get freedom for a bunch of miserable slaves.

The Egyptians finally took Moses seriously when the firstborn of every family in the land was killed, except the firstborn of the Israelites. What happened on that night was an event that was celebrated every year by the Israelites as a remembrance of their great deliverance from the Egyptians. It is the festival of Passover, which is a reminder of how God saved the Hebrews when he struck down the Egyptians.

There is a link between the Passover celebrated by the Jews and the Lord's Supper celebrated by Christians.

Jesus was celebrating the Passover feast with his disciples just before he was betrayed and taken off to be killed.

But the Israelites' escape was not quite yet complete. Pharaoh changed his mind again and sent his soldiers to bring them back. All looked bleak. What chance did they have against the armies of Pharaoh? Many of the Hebrews were suspicious of Moses anyway. They figured it was better to live as slaves in Egypt than to die out in the wilderness.

But a miracle took place at the sea. The Israelites were able to pass safely through the water, and the Egyptians were

trapped and drowned. God had not deserted them. The escape was complete.

What kind of God is this who would bother rescuing a ragged bunch of slaves from one of the great civilizations of the ancient world? It is a God who keeps his promises, who has compassion on the weak and helpless, and who sends a deliverer when we need one. He is the God of Abraham, Isaac, and Jacob, the God of Joseph and Moses, and the God and Father of our Lord Jesus Christ.

We are not through with Moses yet. He remained a leader for 40 years of wandering in the wilderness. The last half of Exodus and the books of Leviticus, Numbers, and Deuteronomy deal in great length with this third period in the life of Moses, especially with his role as lawgiver.

You Shall Not

Why the law?

It seems that someone is always telling us what we are supposed to do. Parents set up rules. Schools set up rules. And in church we hear about rules and laws, too.

We sometimes wonder about all these laws. Some of them seem to be good ones. Some of them don't. What will happen if we break some of them? Will our parents stop loving us? Will we be kicked out of school? Will God do something awful to us, like causing us to get hurt or feel bad or maybe even go to hell? We want to know this especially when we are thinking about God's laws.

Beginning with Exodus 20 and continuing through Leviticus, Numbers, and Deuteronomy the Bible tells about many laws which were given by God to Moses and the Israelites while they were in the wilderness after their escape from Egypt. The movement of the story slows down. There are long interruptions in the action while all kinds of laws are listed. We should keep in mind three general observations about these Old Testament laws.

First, the law is a gift from God to his people in order to help them keep their lives in order. There are some ways of living together in this world that work better than other ways. God does not leave us in the dark to figure all this out for ourselves. He tells us.

If a parent knows that a child will be hurt if she runs into the street, that parent will make a law: "You must not run into the street." If the child obeys, she will be better off than if she does not obey. The parent knows more than the child and it would be a lack of love on the part of the parent not to warn the child of the danger.

Similarly, God gives the law so people will have some idea as to the best way to live. He is not just throwing his weight around because he is God and we are only people. The law is really for our own good.

Second, the relationship of love between God and his people was already there before he gave the law. The purpose of the law is not to get us to be good so God will love us. He already loves us. Before we did anything to deserve that love, he came to us. He made an agreement with Abraham that he would love him and his descendants forever, with no strings attached.

The love of God comes first. He chooses his people first. Then comes the law. The law is to help us live. We are already his people, not because we have kept the law but because he has chosen us.

Third, all of this talk about law assumes that the world makes some sense. And that takes us back to what was said about creation. God made this world. He meant it to be a good place. By our choice, evil entered into the world, so it isn't the way it ought to be. But God is still in control, and through the law

he tells us that things will go better for us if we follow his advice. This is not meant to be a threat, but rather a description of the way life is. Some ways of living will get us into trouble. Other ways are more likely to keep us out of trouble.

If we are open and loving, life will be much more joyful for us than if we are closed off and hostile toward others. If parents are not able to love their child, the child will find difficulty learning to love others. If someone steals, or lies, or commits adultery, that person will get into trouble in one way or another. That is the way life is. What we do with our lives will have a great effect on how our lives turn out.

Having made these general statements about the purpose of laws in the Old Testament, let us look at some examples of the kinds of laws that are found there. Not all of the laws are of the same type. As Christians we have made decisions about these laws and decided that some of them are more important than others, and that some don't apply to us anymore.

Remember that the Bible is both a divine and a human book. It is the record of God's relationship with his people. But some parts of the Bible may have been God's word for a *certain* time and place, not for *every* time and place.

The Ten Commandments
Exodus 20:1-17

The Ten Commandments are the best example of a type of law which is meant to be obeyed for our own good in any time and place. In these laws there are very few specific instructions. Many of them are spoken in negative form: "You shall not do this or that." That is, they set broad limitations on things that we should not do, but they do not spell out the details of what we should do. The details may vary in different societies in different ages, but the broad statement will be true forever.

For example, in any society you must have some kind of laws about the safeguarding of property. "You shall not steal." But there are many different possibilities about how property should be owned or controlled and how it should be bought or sold. There is nothing in this commandment about banks, stock markets, capitalism, socialism, or communism.

Even with these laws which have eternal significance, there are some details which we no longer follow. For example, most

Christians no longer keep the Sabbath. We are still in the spirit of the commandment if we set aside one day a week for worship and rest, but for us that day is Sunday instead of Saturday, the Sabbath. The early Christians began to meet on Sunday, the first day of the week, to celebrate the resurrection of Jesus Christ, and soon Sunday became their holy day.

The Book of the Covenant
Exodus 21:22-36

Chapters 21 to 23 of Exodus are sometimes called the Book of the Covenant. They contain a different kind of law. These laws are about how disputes among members of a particular society are to be resolved. Similar laws are found in other ancient civilizations.

God's people live in the real world and in the real world you need laws to settle disputes and maintain order. God is even concerned about things like oxen that gore people or fall into pits, how slaves should be treated, and what happens when a pregnant woman is hurt during a scuffle between two men. But the specific laws written here no longer apply to us. They were for another time and place.

An example is Exod. 21:23-25 which gives a much-quoted law. It states that if someone injures another person, the punishment given out should be an equal kind of injury. So if a tooth is knocked out, the one responsible for it would have his tooth knocked out.

It could well be that this law was a considerable advancement for its time. It meant that if someone knocked out your tooth, you were not allowed to take his arm or leg or life—only his tooth. That is, it put some restraint on your revenge.

In Matt. 5:38-42, however, Jesus quotes this old law and says that we must now go a step further. In fact, he says, do not seek vengeance at all. Rather be willing to turn the other cheek.

Food laws
Leviticus 11:1-47

Another kind of law in the Old Testament is the food laws found in the book of Leviticus. There are many kinds of animals which were not to be eaten because they were considered unclean. Perhaps there were health problems if some kinds of meat were eaten. One such is pork, which is condemned in Lev. 11:7. With modern ways of preserving food, what was dangerous to eat at one time might be safe now. As you read through this list, you will see that most of these "unclean" foods are things you would not want to eat anyway.

The early church had some discussions about whether or not these food laws still applied to the Gentiles (non-Jews) who were joining the church. (Read about Peter's vision in Acts 10:9-16.) The leaders of the church made the decision that these laws no longer needed to be followed.

There are, then, several kinds of laws in the Old Testament. Some of them still apply to us and some do not. But how are we to make that decision? The problem keeps coming up, not only with Old Testament laws, but also with those in the New Testament. For example, Jesus says that the only kind of divorce allowed is on the ground of unfaithfulness (Matt. 5:32). There are places in Paul's letters where he says that women are to keep silent in church. There are other places that say we should always submit to the government, even when we are certain that it is corrupt and evil.

Are we still to obey these laws? Or can we decide that they (like the laws about what to do when an ox gores a neighbor or what food not to eat) are laws that were meant for that time and do not apply to us? If that is true of some laws, why not others? Are there any laws left? Can they all be explained away?

This is a hard question to answer and one about which there is considerable disagreement. This much we can say. We are not saved by the law, so whether we decide one way or another, it will not affect our salvation or God's love for us. When Jesus was asked which was the greatest commandment, he quoted two Old Testament passages, Deut. 6:5 and Lev. 19:18. These passages say we are to love the Lord with all our heart and soul and mind—and our neighbor as ourselves. Jesus said, "On these two commandments depend all the law and the prophets" (Matt. 22:40).

The specific laws may change from age to age. But it can all be summed up in love for God and neighbor. That is what the law is for—to help us to live in loving relationship with God and our fellow human beings. Any specific laws must be judged by that standard of love.

The Conquest of Canaan

Grumbling in the wilderness
Numbers 11–14

The Israelites willingly followed Moses out of Egypt. Certainly the wilderness couldn't be worse than slavery in Egypt. But they were soon complaining.

Even after the spectacular wonders and miracles that happened in Egypt, even after the giving of the law on Mt. Sinai, even with a leader as great as Moses, the people still complained and fussed about hunger and thirst and bugs and sickness. They didn't want to be out there in the wilderness. They wanted to be in a land of their own.

It took a while before they got there. Their goal was the promised land, the land where Abraham and Jacob had lived before, the land of Canaan where Abraham went when God called him from his home in Mesopotamia. But they lost their nerve and God lost his patience and told them that because of their lack of trust in him, they would have to wander in the wilderness for 40 years. Only Caleb and Joshua survived those years. All the other adults who had come out of Egypt, including Moses, would be dead before the Israelites finally entered the promised land.

Rule by judges

If the Israelites were to develop as a people and become a blessing, they had to have that promised land. The big problem was that the land God had promised them was already occupied. If Israel was going to move in, someone else would have to move out. This meant some people were going to be forced out of their homes and many would be killed. So the stories in Joshua, Judges, and 1 Samuel are problems for us because they talk about invasion, war, killing, and a God who seems to support that kind of thing.

After 40 years in the wilderness, the Israelites ended up on the east side of Palestine. Moses died and Joshua became the leader. They crossed the Jordan and captured a few key cities.

The process of how they took over the land is a little hazy, but it was probably something like this. First they moved into the hill country in central Palestine. It was not heavily populated. Then they defeated some cities and settled down in some unoccupied areas. There were still many Canaanite cities that were not defeated, and for about 200 years there was constant turmoil and unrest. This was the period of the judges.

The book of Judges and the early chapters of 1 Samuel tell about this unsteady 200-year period. The Israelites were hanging on to pieces of land here and there, surrounded by enemies. There was no strong central government to unite them and give them strength, but instead they depended on God to provide a leader when an enemy threatened their survival.

And that is what God did. There was Ehud, the left-handed hero from the tribe of Benjamin, who killed the fat king of Moab in the bathroom (Judges 3:15-30). Deborah was a judge who rallied the tribes against the Canaanite kings (Judges 4–5). Gideon defeated Midian with a handful of troops and the support of the Lord and probably could have become king if he had wanted to (Judges 6–8). And Jephthah was a kind of Robin Hood judge, a semi-outlaw type who ended up tragically sacrificing his daughter to fulfill a vow (Judges 11–12). The judge Samson had great strength, a love for beautiful women, a hatred of the Philistines, and perhaps not the sharpest mind in Israel (Judges 13–16). And finally there was Samuel, who was the last of the judges and the first of the prophets (1 Samuel 1–3).

The problem of war
Joshua 6:1-21

The books of Joshua and Judges pose several questions that have no easy answers. One of them has to do with war.

Jericho was the first key city captured by the Israelites after they crossed the Jordan into Palestine. The story they told about this capture is an example of what could be called "holy war." God had already decided that Israel would win the battle. All they had to do was trust him and follow directions. It did not matter that they were outnumbered. If they trusted in God as they went into battle, there was no way they could lose.

So the story as we have it is a miracle. There is no way to explain it away. The marching around the city, the use of rams' horns, and the mighty shout were enough to make the residents of Jericho so frightened that when Israel finally attacked on the seventh day, they were petrified with fear. And the walls came tumbling down.

The Israelites did not take any hostages. All the people and animals were destroyed by the sword as an offering to God. Then the Israelites burned the city and saved only the gold and silver and other metal vessels which were taken for the treasury of the house of the Lord.

Some people are embarrassed by this story and wish it were not in the Bible. Some have tried to explain that this kind of cruelty represents a primitive time before people knew about a God of love. Later on they would grow in their understanding and not think of God as a God of war anymore.

Such an explanation is only partly right. God was a God of love to the Hebrews and made promises to them and had compassion on them. But he is also a God who fights against the evil in our world. If he is concerned about the good, it means he is concerned about removing the evil. And many of the nations of that time were evil. The powers of evil are too much for us to handle without his help.

By contrast, in the New Testament, Jesus tells us to love our enemies, to turn the other cheek. He did not fight back, but submitted to evil men who killed him on the cross. How do we fit these ideas together? On the one hand, we see evil which must be defeated. On the other hand, we are supposed to overcome evil with good.

As Christians, we have not been able to solve this to everyone's satisfaction. Some Christians are pacifists. They think that war and using force is always wrong. Others say that we must

sometimes fight evil or we will all be overcome. They argue that we must use good judgment in deciding which battles God wants us to fight and which ones we should stay out of and let God handle.

There are no easy answers, and there is a lot of disagreement on this issue. Was it right for the United States to fight in World War II or the war in Vietnam? There were Christians on both sides of the question.

Is it right for one group to take away the land of another group? In the story of Joshua, God seemed to want that for his people for the long-range benefit of the world. What about the European immigrants who took the American continent from the Indians? What about the struggle still going on between Jews and Arabs for this same land for which Joshua fought?

The problem of justice

Judges 2:6–3:15

Another problem concerns justice. In telling the history of their nation, the writers of Judges give their explanation for the good and bad things that happened to them during this diffi- cult 200-year period of time. When bad things happened it was because the people had sinned and worshiped other gods. When God sent a judge to help them, it was because he had heard their cry for help and took pity on them. According to this view, people suffer for their sins and are rewarded when they wor- ship the true God in the right way.

But does it always work out this neatly? Are the good always rewarded? Do the bad always get punished? This question will come up again in our Bible study.

But in each of these stories from Judges we see the same pattern repeated. The people turn away from God, he punishes them by sending an enemy to have power over them, the people cry out for help, God takes pity and sends a deliverer. After the judge dies they return to their evil ways and the cycle is repeated once again.

Enter the king

At the end of this period of the judges, Israel decided to try a dangerous new experiment. There was no strong central gov- ernment; instead, the people thought of God as being their ruler. When they needed help, God would send someone. They seemed to distrust human rulers. This might have been the result of the years of their living under tyranny in Egypt.

But by the time of Samuel, the threat from enemy nations was so severe that drastic action was necessary. Samuel became the spokesman for God in choosing a king. The stories about this in 1 Samuel 8–11 show that there was a lot of uncertainty about whether this was really a good idea or not, but he finally picked Saul to be the king.

From this time on there was a new phase in the history of the people of Israel. They were no longer a collection of loose- ly knit tribes. Now, under Saul, David, and Solomon, they were established as a nation in the land God had promised Abraham hundreds of years before.

Three Kings and Two Prophets

The search for a king

If you were choosing a king, what kind of person would you look for? You wouldn't expect him to be perfect. But you would want someone who could admit when he was wrong and would try to do better. You would want someone you could trust and respect. And surely you would want someone who was able to defend your country from its enemies.

The ideal king would care about each citizen. He would rule with justice and not give special deals just because someone had money or power. He would watch out for the poor, the orphans, dependent mothers, the sick, and others who couldn't take care of themselves. It would help if he had personal charm, good looks, and the ability to talk before crowds of people.

These were the traits that the Israelites were looking for in a king. Some of the old-timers were doubtful they would ever find such a leader, and they thought it would be better not to have a king at all. They argued that God had always sent judges when the going got rough, so why shouldn't they keep on trusting him to do that.

Other people had what they considered a more "realistic" view of things. It was fine to talk about trusting God to send a leader, but "God helps those who help themselves." When the Philistines are threatening to take over your country, it is ridiculous to sit around waiting for God to send someone to save you. Get organized. Pick a leader. Give him some power and protect yourself.

In some ways, the story of Israel for the next several hundred years was the search for that perfect king who would give the nation the kind of leadership they wanted and needed. Most of the time they were disappointed, and, as we shall see, there came a time when there was no king at all. Then they began to look ahead to the future, when God would finally send the kind of king they had always hoped for.

The disappointing king
1 Samuel 9 and 16

Saul was the first king. He was a handsome young man and apparently a good soldier. While looking for some of his father's lost animals, he came in contact with Samuel, who was a seer. A seer was a kind of fortune-teller. Samuel informed Saul that God had chosen him to be the first king (1 Samuel 10).

In those days, when someone was made king, oil was poured on his head. Therefore the king was "the one who is anointed." The Hebrew word for this is *messiah,* and the Greek word is *christ.* The king, then, was called the "messiah" or "christ."

Saul was a disappointing king. He was very moody and often depressed. Sometimes he had the idea that everyone was out to get him. This caused him to lose support. He even lost the support of Samuel who had anointed him king in the first place.

Samuel was the spokesman for God. He was probably the first of those Old Testament people that we call prophets. One of his jobs was to keep an eye on the king to be sure that he stayed honest and was obedient to God. When Saul lost favor with Samuel, it was time to choose a new king. God already had his eye on a young man who would become the greatest king that Israel ever had—David.

The greatest king
1 Samuel 17; 2 Samuel 7:1-17; 11:1–12:15

Most of the rest of 1 Samuel is about the rise of David and the decline of Saul. David came to Saul's attention because he was skillful at playing the lyre, "a man of valor, a man of war, prudent in speech, and a man of good presence" (1 Sam. 16:18). David became famous after his battle with the Philistine giant, Goliath (1 Samuel 17). As a result of David's fame, Saul became jealous of him. David had to run away to save his life.

Saul chased him around the countryside but was not able to kill him.

Eventually the Philistines killed both Saul and his son Jonathan. David, the popular hero and warrior, was chosen to be king. He was a warm, sentimental man who was deeply saddened when Saul and Jonathan were killed. In 2 Sam. 1:17-27 there is a beautiful piece of ancient poetry which is a lament that David sang when his dear friend Jonathan died. David was a musician and a poet, and the tradition developed in later times that he wrote many of the psalms.

After the death of Saul, David took action to unify the country and to defeat the Philistines. He captured Jerusalem, which was one of those Canaanite cities that still had not been captured by Israel, and made it his capital. From that time till the present, Jerusalem has been an important city.

David hoped to build a temple at Jerusalem (read 2 Sam. 7:1-17), and consulted with the prophet Nathan about this. At first, Nathan thought it would be all right, but then he had a dream in which God told him that David was not to build a temple. God had something better for David. He made a promise to David. He promised that someone from David's family would always be the king. He would never take the kingship away from David as he had done with Saul. The kingship of David would last forever.

This important passage is the beginning of the hope for a new kind of king or messiah. We call this a messianic hope. When the day came that there were no more kings in Israel, the people would look into the future for a new son of David who would be sent from God to deliver them and become an ideal king. Jesus was that long-awaited son of David. When Christians tell the stories about Jesus' birth, they point out that he was descended from David (Matt. 1:1-16 and Luke 3:23-31).

Most of the rest of the story of David in 2 Samuel is downhill (read 2 Sam. 11:1-17 and 12:1-15). David was attracted to a beautiful woman named Bathsheba, whose husband was off fighting in the war. Before long David found out that she was going to have a baby and he was the father. He summoned her husband, Uriah, to come home and be with his wife so that it would look like he was the father. But Uriah refused to enjoy the comforts of being home with his wife when fellow soldiers had to camp in the field. So in order to protect his own reputation, David arranged to have Uriah killed in battle.

The greatest king in Israel's history committed adultery and murder. And the Bible tells the whole story. There is no cover-up. Once again we see that even the great people in the Bible were capable of doing ugly things.

Then God sent the prophet Nathan to David to tell him of his punishment. In a sense, God was still the ruler, because the human ruler had to answer to him. He was looking out for his people. From that time on, David's life was one unhappy episode after another. His children murdered each other. His favorite son, Absalom, led a rebellion and was killed. Finally, his sons Adonijah and Solomon schemed and plotted to see which would be king when David died.

The prophet Nathan did two things in this story. He brought promises from God and he brought warnings from God. He was concerned with justice and fair government. There would be many more prophets later in the Old Testament. They would be concerned with these same things.

The wise king

1 Kings 3:1-28

David's son, Solomon, was also a great king. But the biblical stories about him are a bit different from the ones about David. They do not tell us what was going on inside Solomon. They tend to glorify him and talk about his great reputation rather than to tell of his human side. It is easier to feel affectionate toward David than toward Solomon.

Solomon was famous for a number of things: the temple he built which David had not been allowed to build, his 1000 wives (it was the custom when you made a treaty with another king to marry one of his daughters), and his fabulous wealth.

Solomon was also remembered as being a wise man. The way he decided which of two women was the real mother of a baby they both claimed is an example of his wisdom. Because of his reputation as a wise man, later tradition held that Solomon was the author of some of the biblical wisdom books like Proverbs, Ecclesiastes, and the Song of Solomon.

In later times, the people of Israel looked back on this period as the good old days. Under David and Solomon, their nation

Solomon discovers the baby's mother

was stronger and more unified than it would ever be again. This was a glorious time in their history. In a similar way, we often look back and think that things were probably better in our country back in the "good old days."

David was the ideal king. Every king who came after him was compared with him and was judged to be not quite as good. In spite of his weaknesses, he was remembered fondly as the good king who submitted himself to God and repented and took his punishment when he was caught doing something wrong.

Solomon was a great king, too. He accomplished much and was looked on with pride as one who had made Israel great in the eyes of the rest of the world. But Solomon, too, had his weaknesses. He put people to work as slave laborers. He taxed them so that they had hardly any money left. By the time he died, there was so much dissatisfaction that the strong, united country was soon divided by rebellion.

In summary, let us look at a few important points to remember from the stories of Saul, David, and Solomon:

1. God wants us to have a stable, fair government. Earthly kings are subject to God and his rule; if they forget that, there will be trouble.

2. The hope for an ideal king begins with David. He is the model of the good king. God made him a promise that his descendants would always be on the throne, and the Jews still had this hope in their hearts at the time Jesus arrived on the scene.

3. Again we see that the Bible is full of stories about human beings who are less than perfect. We are once more reminded that we are not saved by what we do, but by God's action. God loves us even though we are disobedient. He will not abandon us.

4. In these stories of the early kings, we see the same idea of history that we saw in the book of Judges. The world made sense. There was a reason why Saul failed as king. There was a reason why David had all that trouble with his family. There was a reason why the kingdom split after the death of Solomon. God is in control. He makes sure everything comes out right in the end.

5. This was the time of the beginning of people called prophets. They were spokesmen for God. They stood for justice. They brought promises to the king that God would be with him. They also brought warnings of what would happen if the king should be disobedient.

The Big Split

A kingdom divided

1 Kings 12:1-15

King Solomon's policies led to trouble. Israel could have remained a strong and important nation, and could have been God's blessing to other nations. But that was not to be.

After Solomon's death, his son, Rehoboam, became the king. He could have had the support of his people if he had been willing to lighten the burdens that Solomon had laid on them. That is what the old men advised him to do. But the young men told him to demand even more from the people—to show them who was king. This was exactly the kind of arrogance of power that some folks had warned against before Israel chose the first king, Saul.

The result of Rehoboam's unbending attitude was a split in the nation. The people in the north refused to accept the grandson of David as their king. They declared themselves an independent country and set up a man named Jeroboam as their king.

In the rest of the two books of Kings, the story of God's people is the story of two kingdoms. The Northern Kingdom is called Israel, and the Southern Kingdom is called Judah. Now, instead of one reasonably strong nation, there were two small, weak ones wasting their energy fighting each other. It is not hard to see why later generations looked back on the time of David and Solomon as the good old days.

The story in the books of Kings jumps back and forth between these two countries. We read about Israel for a while and then jump back to Judah. There are many details about some kings and hardly any about others. The Northern Kingdom of Israel lasted for some 200 years after the death of Solomon. It fell about 722 B.C. The Southern Kingdom of Judah, with its capital at Jerusalem, lasted another 135 years. It fell about 586 or 587 B.C.

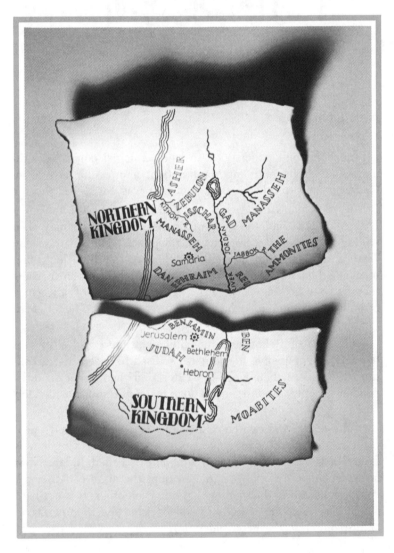

There were a few good times in the history of these two nations. But most of the story is a gloomy tale of one bad king after another, continual unfaithfulness to God, constant wars, and final defeat and exile.

It is not a pretty story for a people who claimed to be God's chosen people. It makes you wonder. If God allows his own people to suffer like that, what does he do with others? It made the Israelites and the Jews (Jews are people from Judah) wonder about God. They wrote about such questions in books that became part of our Bible.

It is impossible for us to talk about everything in the two books of Kings. Let us concentrate on two chapters that will give us examples of the kind of stories that are written here. 1 Kings 17 deals with Elijah. 2 Kings 17 tries to explain why the Northern Kingdom was defeated by the Assyrians.

Elijah's miracles
1 Kings 17:1-24

Scattered among the stories of kings, sins, and wars in 1 and 2 Kings, we have some stories of prophets who gave promises and warnings. The most important of these prophets was Elijah. There are stories about him in 1 Kings 17–21 and 2 Kings 1–2.

We first meet Elijah in 1 Kings 17, where we are told about three miracles. First, he was fed by ravens in the wilderness. Then a widow's oil and flour never ran out. And finally, he restored life to the dead son of the widow. Notice the similarities between these Old Testament stories about Elijah and the New Testament stories about Jesus. Jesus, too, spent time alone in the wilderness. He, too, provided more than enough food from only a little food—a few loaves of bread and pieces of fish. And he, too, raised people from the dead.

Elijah was an important figure to the early Christians. The last two verses in the Old Testament, Mal. 4:5-6, tell how Elijah will come again before the end of the world. The New Testament reports that some people thought John the Baptist was Elijah come back to life. Some even thought Jesus was Elijah. Remember when Jesus was transfigured on the mountain? Two Old Testament characters were with him—Moses and Elijah (Luke 9:28-36).

Elijah's death was special. He was taken directly to heaven in a whirlwind, and when his followers looked for his body, they couldn't find it (2 Kings 2:1-18). People wondered what kind of special plan God had in mind for Elijah. Some expected his return to announce the coming of a new age. When the Christians became convinced that Jesus had come to bring in a new age, they naturally thought of Elijah. So the way they told the story about Jesus was affected by what they knew about Elijah.

This is not the first time we have run into events that seemed impossible. There was the birth of a child to parents almost 100 years old, the bush that wouldn't burn in the fire, the plagues that God sent against Egypt, the parting of the sea to let Israel through, the tumbling of the walls of Jericho. And now these stories about Elijah.

There are three places in the Bible that tell of many miracles —the time of the exodus, the time of Elijah (and Elisha who comes right after him), and the time of Jesus.

Because it is hard to believe something for which we cannot find a logical answer, many people don't know what to do with the miracle stories of the Bible. There are at least three possibilities. One is that we can accept the stories at face value. After all, God is God. If he wants to do something out of the ordinary, no one can tell him he can't do it.

Or you can try to give some logical explanation for the miracle. For example, you might say that the boy in 1 Kings 17:17-24 was never really dead. He only looked as though he were dead. And when Elijah stretched himself out on top of the child, he was actually giving him mouth-to-mouth resuscitation. You can say that. But it really doesn't answer all the problems.

The third thing you can do is to admit there is a mystery about the work of God in the world. We can't possibly know all there is to know about him. So stop worrying about whether something happened exactly as described in the Bible. Instead, concentrate on trying to understand what the story tells us about God. Where God is especially active with his presence and power in the world, we have a miracle story to drive home that point. God wants us to have life rather than death, and he has the power to defeat death. That's what the miracle of Elijah and the widow's son is about.

Israel's fall

2 Kings 17:1-23

The people who were writing this history in 2 Kings believed there were reasons for Israel's defeat. God would not turn his back on his people without some reason. And 2 Kings 17, after describing the details of what happened, tries to explain why it happened. Some things to notice in this chapter are:

1. The exodus is remembered as the great event that showed most clearly God's love and mercy.

2. Trouble came not because God changed but because his people were unfaithful to him.

3. God was very angry with Israel. This makes us uncomfortable and questions arise. Does God get angry over little things as well as big things? How long does he stay angry? Will he forgive us again? Will he ever get angry enough to cut us off from him forever? There were times when the people of Israel might have thought so. But we as Christians have learned that the forgiving love of God is without limit.

4. God was not punishing Israel without some warning. They knew what to expect if they were disobedient. They had the law, prophets, and seers to warn them of the consequences of disobedience. But they did not listen. So the disaster occurred.

5. It was the kings of Israel who were especially to blame. They caused Israel to sin. Jeroboam started it. David had his faults, but he never turned his people away from the true God and toward other gods. The rulers of the Northern Kingdom were not descendants of David. God had not made the same kind of promise to them that he had made to David.

6. Note the phrase "until this day" in verse 23. That little phrase tells us that this interpretation of the history was written some time after Israel went into exile. The writer was looking back on this tragic event and trying to explain as best he could why such a thing would happen. He thought he had the matter solved. Israel sinned and was punished, but God was still working through the Southern Kingdom of Judah.

An even more difficult test of faith and harder question to answer came later when Judah fell. As long as Judah survived there was hope that God's promises would be fulfilled. But what happens when Judah, too, is defeated and carried into exile?

Gloomy Prophets

Repent and return to God

Imagine that it is Christmas morning and you are in church. You've had a good Christmas Eve and received many presents. The church is beautifully decorated and everyone seems so happy. Christmas is such a great time of the year.

Suddenly, in the middle of the sermon, a stranger that you have never seen before gets up and starts yelling at the pastor. He runs down the center aisle to the front of the church. The poor pastor doesn't know what to do. He stands speechless, staring at the intruder.

The stranger begins to preach. But it is not sweet talk about the baby Jesus. Rather, he points his finger and says we ought to be ashamed of ourselves for spending so much money on Christmas presents when there are people starving to death in our community. He says that God is angry with us because we are concerned only about ourselves. We are phonies and God will not listen to our prayers or songs until we take care of those who are lonely or poor or jobless. His message is, "Repent and return to God."

Finally, the pastor regains his composure. He signals for three of the biggest ushers he can find. They grab the man, remove him from church as quickly as possible, and he is put in jail overnight. You agree that it certainly serves him right for having ruined a beautiful Christmas service.

Something like this happened in Old Testament times. People like Amos and Isaiah and Jeremiah made absolute pests of themselves. They appeared at the most awkward times, often in the middle of a solemn service, and warned the people they could not hide behind their fancy talk about God. Pointing their fingers, they declared that God would punish the people for their empty words and evil lives. The people in those days did not appreciate such warnings any more than we would if someone directed them at us.

What is a prophet?

The Bible calls such individuals prophets. A prophet is one who claims to have a special message from God; he won't rest until he speaks that message. We have already met some of the prophets—people like Samuel, Nathan, and Elijah. Their stories are in the historical books of Samuel and Kings. But there are later prophets whose words are recorded in books that are named after them: Isaiah, Jeremiah, Ezekiel, Hosea, Amos, and others.

Like the early ones, these later prophets had both good and bad messages for the people. God responds to his people according to what is best for them. If they are discouraged and feel helpless, then he sends a good word to remind them of his love that will never let them go. If they are forgetting him, hurting others, bringing trouble on themselves, then he sends a word to try to help them see what they are doing so there can be a change.

In this chapter we want to think about the prophets with the gloomy messages, the ones who warned about bad things in the future. Most of these prophets spoke their harsh words before the fall of Israel or Judah. In 2 Kings 17 we read how God sent these prophets to give warnings. But they were not listened to.

In regard to these prophets, let's consider three questions: (1) How do people know if the prophet is really from God and not just a troublemaker? (2) Why does God send prophets with messages of doom? (3) Is there any hope after doom comes?

Is he from God?

How do we know a prophet is really from God? For example, was our Christmas intruder from God or was he merely acting on his own? How can prophets be so bold as to make the claim to know something that other people don't know? How can they talk with such certainty, as if they got the message directly from God himself?

Almost all the prophets in the Bible had trouble convincing their listeners they were really sent by God. Often they got into arguments with other people who claimed to be prophets, but whose message was completely different. For example, in Jeremiah 28 we read that Jeremiah got into an argument with a prophet named Hananiah. Hananiah kept telling people that there was going to be peace and everything was going to be all right. Jeremiah was predicting bad things. But since people usually would rather hear good news, more of them believed Hananiah than Jeremiah.

It was Jeremiah's prophecy that proved to be correct. Hananiah was probably just as sincere as Jeremiah. He also believed in God. He may even have been convinced that God had spoken to him and that it was his duty to speak against the negative pessimism of Jeremiah. But it was true then, as it is now, that only time reveals who the true prophet is.

In order to convince others of the truth of their calling, most of the Old Testament prophets wrote about the experience of their call. Hosea wrote how God told him to marry a prostitute, to divorce her, and then remarry her (Hosea 1–3). Amos probably became convinced of his calling after a series of visions (Amos 7:1-9). Isaiah had a remarkable experience in the temple with strange creatures flying around and God talking to him directly (Isa. 6:1-8). Jeremiah did not have such a supernatural kind of experience, but had the feeling that God had called him for his task even before he was born (Jer. 1:4-10).

Each had a direct experience with God that convinced him that he must speak out. But each experience was different. God calls different prophets in different ways. We cannot tell the true prophet from the false one by the kind of experience he has. Some will have spectacular visions of God, like Isaiah. Most will grow into an awareness of God's plan for them more slowly, like Jeremiah.

Why doom?
Amos 5:14-15; Ezekiel 2:1-5

The most important reason for sending prophets with a message of doom is the one we have already mentioned. God wants us to repent, change our ways, live better with each other, and trust him. Even though the prophet brought a description of bad things that would happen, there was a chance those things would not happen if people repented. Amos 5:14-15 is an example of this call to repent.

The problem was the poor response to the prophet when he tried to get people to change. People preferred to listen to Hananiah rather than Jeremiah. Then the prophet began to wonder what his purpose was if no one was going to repent. He became discouraged and no longer expected his words to have any effect in bringing about change.

In such cases, the prophet's words were an announcement of

what was going to happen rather than a call to change. But he still felt that words from God must be spoken. Later generations would know that God had sent warnings and perhaps they would then be able to understand what went wrong. Ezek. 2:1-5 expresses this thought.

As strange as it may sound, God sent prophets of doom to his people because he loved them. He cares enough to say a harsh word to us because it is for our own good. It is not easy to say hard words to someone you love. Nor is it easy to be critical when you want to say nice things. But it is important to speak the truth. You cannot pretend everything is fine when it isn't. If friends are going to hurt themselves or someone else because of the way they live, then we should speak out. God did this through his prophets.

Is there any hope?
Amos 8; Hosea 11

Some of the Old Testament prophets were very pessimistic. They almost talked as if there were no hope for God's people. Amos, especially, talked like that. You get the feeling from reading Chapter 8 that God had completely given up on his people. The last words of the chapter say that "they shall fall, and never rise again." Perhaps Amos was exaggerating in a last desperate effort to get people to hear his warning. Perhaps he really did believe what he said was going to happen. He was addressing the Northern Kingdom of Israel, and, as it turned out, his words were true. The kingdom of Israel, after being defeated by Assyria in 722 B.C., never did rise again.

Most of these prophets of doom did maintain some hope, however. Hosea 11 is a good example of this. In this chapter God was speaking through the prophet and thinking about his past relationships with his people. In spite of all he had done for them, they had not been true to him. But he could not bring himself to cut them off completely.

God remembered his love for his people and his promises to them. Even the disaster that the prophets were expecting would not be the end. There would be new beginnings. God is not like human beings who get disgusted and turn away from those they used to love. God will never do that. Instead he promises a new and more glorious day.

Hope in the Midst of Disaster

▮ The painful exile

It is easy to believe in God when everything goes well. When you live in a rich country, your parents have good jobs, your family is in good health, you don't feel depressed, your country is not at war, and your team wins the big games—then it is easy to believe there is some power for good that is watching out for us and making everything turn out all right.

But how about when unpleasant or even tragic things happen in your life? What if a parent or brother or sister gets sick? Or dies? Or you get sick? Or what if you feel unhappy and lonely all the time? What if nothing ever seems to turn out right for you? Then what? Do you still believe in God?

Since the time of Abraham, God's people had kept going by remembering God's promises. If the going got rough, they reminded themselves that God would never break his promises. This helped them look ahead to better times.

However, there was one event which was so terribly disastrous that it nearly destroyed God's people. It was a time of shattered hopes. Things they thought could never happen to them did happen. Thus they were forced to rethink what they believed.

This event was the exile. The Northern Kingdom of Israel had been destroyed in 722 B.C. But as long as Judah survived, there was hope that God's message would get out to the whole world. The people in Judah learned from Israel's fate and continued to survive for another 135 years as a country. Descendants of David remained on the throne, though some of them were terrible kings, especially a man named Manasseh.

A grandson of Manasseh, Josiah, became king of Judah about 640 B.C. He was probably the best king since David. He ruled with justice and got rid of foreign control in government and pagan influence in religion. There seemed to be a wave of optimism in the land. God was with them. He had sent them a god-fearing and fair ruler. There was a religious revival in the nation which the people expected would lead to a long time of peace and prosperity.

But it didn't happen that way. Within a few years, Josiah was killed in battle and those who ruled after him were weak and ineffective kings. Josiah's reforms didn't last. By 587 B.C., Judah was destroyed by the Babylonians. The king was sent away to Babylon along with most of the leaders, and Jerusalem, including the palace and temple, was a heap of ruins. God's people were scattered. The king was gone. The center of worship was gone. Things had been rough before, but never like this. And the letdown was even greater because they had expected so much after Josiah.

So the scattered people of Judah had to think about what all this meant. The story was not working out the way they had expected, and there were all kinds of questions. They were in the same kind of situation that the followers of Jesus would be in a few hundred years later when the man they called king was suddenly dead.

In this chapter we shall look at some of the biblical writings from around the time of the fall of Jerusalem and a little later. These writings raise some very difficult questions.

Is God all-powerful?
Isaiah 45:18-25

"Is our God really all-powerful? Why were his people defeated if he is such a powerful God? It appears that the god of the Babylonians is the greatest god because his side won." Some of the Jews were probably tempted to think like this. Those who went into exile were soon aware that Babylon made Jerusalem look like the second-rate capital of a third-rate country. Could the God of a third-rate country that had just been wiped off the earth still claim to be the God of the whole universe?

The last part of the book of Isaiah was probably written during the exile in answer to questions like these. The author tried to renew the people's hope and to convince them there was no other god than the God who had led them from the beginning. Salvation, deliverance, and a return to their land was possible. There could be a second exodus like the first one. But this salvation could come only from God, the one who made heaven and earth. His name is Yahweh (translated "the Lord" in the RSV), and there is no other. He is still in control.

Can God be trusted?
Habakkuk 1:12—2:4

But can our God still be trusted? He had promised that Abraham was to be the father of a mighty nation that would bless all people. He had promised that a son of David would always be king of Judah. But now there was no nation. Did God break his promises? Was he just fooling? Is he just like human beings who finally give up on someone after they have been disappointed several times? Can we still trust him?

There are many efforts to deal with this question in the Bible. One of the best places to look is in the little book of Habakkuk. The author saw that Judah was about to be crushed by Babylon. He realized that God was using Babylon to judge Judah. But it bothered him that Babylon was even worse than Judah. Judah was guilty, but Babylon was even more guilty. How could God let that go on? And for how long?

Habakkuk asked these questions and then went up to a tower

and waited for God to answer. The answer was, "Take it easy, Habakkuk. It is going to take time. Wait. But in the meantime, trust me. The righteous person will just have to live in faithfulness until I make everything right again."

This answer doesn't solve everything. But it does say that God can still be trusted. He says, "You don't understand why all these awful things are happening now. But if you can just hang in there and keep trusting me, I will take care of it." Some of the Jews were able to accept this. Others were not.

Can we survive in exile?
Ezekiel 10:18-19; 11:22-25

"Can we survive without a king? Can we worship without a temple? Can we exist without our own country?" These were hard questions in the minds of the exiled Jews, questions all tied to the previous promises that we have talked about.

The Jews found they could survive even though they were scattered all over the world with no government of their own and no central place of worship. They put the promises of God in cold storage for a while. They decided the promises were still true, but they would be fulfilled at a later time. They were encouraged by the fact that the king was still alive in Babylon and being treated well. This story is told in 2 Kings 25:27-31.

Ezekiel, a priest as well as a prophet, had a vision in which he saw the glory of God leave the temple before it was destroyed. He found that God could still be worshiped even by those in exile. God was not confined to the temple. But the temple would someday be rebuilt and the glory of the Lord would return there once again.

So they lived in hope that God would again bring them back to their land, give them a new king, and help them build a new temple.

When will the punishment end?
Jeremiah 14:19-22; Lamentations 5

As time went on, the Jews became more and more impatient with their situation. They cried out to God for relief. Habakkuk had been told by God to wait and to trust in him. But for how long? What was the purpose of suffering any longer? God had made his point. The prophets of doom were right. The punish-

ment made some sense. But now what? When would the punishment end? If God was going to give relief, why didn't he do it?

These are the kinds of questions spoken to God in the laments of Jeremiah and others. A lament is a cry of mourning at a funeral. It is what is said in sadness when someone has died. It is what is said when the country dies. It is a cry of despair directed to God.

One final thing to remember in all of this—it is all right to ask such questions. There is no question so out of line that you should not ask it. The people who wrote the Bible asked God some hard questions. They did not hold back out of fear that questions showed lack of faith or respect. They knew God wanted them to be honest with him and with themselves. There is no way you can grow in understanding or faith if you do not ask the questions that need asking.

At the time of the exile in the Old Testament or the time of the crucifixion in the New Testament, it was hard to see God at work in the world. There are similar times in our own lives. But the Bible tells us that he is present, working with us, even in those difficult times when it is the hardest to believe this.

79

Living in Hope

What the world needs now

There is a song that says, "What the world needs now is love." Many people would agree. If we could just learn how to get along with one another, that would make for a wonderful world in which to live.

How would you respond to a poll taker who wanted to know your opinion about what this world needs most? Of course your answer would depend on your background and the way things are going for you right now. Some would say that everything is going well, and would hope for no sudden changes that would take away some of the good things they already have. Others would want many changes because of the difficult circumstances in their own lives and in the world around them.

Maybe what our world needs is another George Washington or Abraham Lincoln or Winston Churchill. When present leaders fail us, those great leaders of the past look very good. If only another Washington or Lincoln would come on the scene and take charge and solve our national and world problems!

The Jews in exile found themselves longing for a better world. They barely survived the catastrophe of the exile. Many of them were killed. Those who did survive had many painful questions. But once they realized God was still with them and they were not going to disappear as a people, they began to hope again. They were at rock bottom and there was no place to go but up. What would God do next? What did the world need most of all?

80

Those special messengers from God, the prophets, came with a new kind of message. They no longer spoke of doom. Those awful words of an earlier time had come true. Now was a time when God sought to comfort his people. Now was a time to speak of new beginnings. Even prophets like Jeremiah and Ezekiel, who had been very hard-nosed earlier, were now gentle, optimistic, and supporting.

Of course, all of these prophets did not think, talk, or write in the same way. They had different ideas of what God ought to do next in order to set things right again. Just as our modern poll taker would get many opinions of what the world needs most, so the prophets in the Old Testament gave different ideas of what the future would bring.

Let us briefly list some of the kinds of hope that are found in the Old Testament prophets. They will be listed in an order that moves from hopes that are very realistic and down to earth, to those that are more idealistic and less down to earth.

The hope for a Messiah
Isaiah 9:6-7; 11:1-5; Zechariah 9:9-10

"What we reallly need is a new king. He must be like David, who has become the example of what a king should be. The terrible event of the exile would not have happened if there had been good leadership in Israel and Judah. If we had some-

one who was an ideal king instead of a loser or a crook, then we could have our own nation again. The new king could defeat our enemies, rule with justice, and watch out for those who are weak. We could trust him and life could go on as before, only better. He would be called *messiah* in Hebrew, or *christ* in Greek, because he would be the one who was anointed."

This view is not unlike the view of someone who would like to see another Lincoln or Churchill. What we want is someone who has both strength to protect us and compassion to be concerned for our needs. Not every leader has these qualities.

▨ The hope for the Messianic Age
Isaiah 61:1-4

"What we need is a life free from trouble, unhappiness, and slavery. Then we will have the kind of world God promised, when he finally removes all things that make us sad or sick. There is no point in just talking about a king or Messiah. Our whole lives need to be different. If a good king will help that situation, so much the better."

This hope is more concerned with the new quality of life that is necessary rather than what kind of persons we need as leaders. In Isa. 61:1, the prophet got up and said that God had *anointed* him to speak this message of hope. *Anointed* has the same root as the word *messiah*, but in this case it was a prophet who was anointed and not a king.

According to Luke 4:16-21, Jesus read from this Isaiah text in the synagogue in Nazareth when he began his ministry. And he told them that this scripture passage was being fulfilled in their midst that very day. Jesus identified himself with a hope that talked about a life free from pain and affliction, though he was reluctant to talk about himself as a glorious new king like David.

▨ The hope for religious leadership
Ezekiel 43:1-12

"What we need is to return to our own land and set up a new kind of government where the people in charge will be priests instead of politicians. It is obvious that the kings have failed us. They were not responsive to the will of God, even though God had sent them enough prophets to warn them. You can't trust kings and other politicians. Power corrupts. So when we get a new chance, we should be ruled by the religious leaders. They are closer to God and will inspire us to live in such a way that a disaster like the exile will not happen again."

This was the view of the prophet Ezekiel. In Chapters 40 to 48 of his book, he presents the ideal society as one in which the priest is more important than the prince. This view has appeared again and again in history and led to a struggle between the powers of the religious establishment and the powers of the state. Most of us today would not think a society ruled by priests, or even pastors, would be the best of all possible worlds.

The hope of a new covenant
Jeremiah 31:31-34

What the world really needs is individuals who are different, who are changed, who know what they are supposed to do, and do it.

Jeremiah looked forward to the new day when God would make a "new covenant" with his people. (Another way to say "new covenant" is to say "new testament." From this we get the names of the two parts of our Bible—the Old and New Testaments.) In this new age, no one will have to be told what to do. We will not need prophets preaching the law to people. There will be no force. No one will have to be scared into obedience. No one will feel guilty. Every person will simply know what is right to do, and will do it.

This is a beautiful hope; what a wonderful world it would be! But how will it happen? This seems more idealistic, less practical, than talk about kings and priests and society. How do people get to the point of really wanting to live with God's law written in their hearts? How do they change? The prophets couldn't get them to change. Only God can bring about such a dramatic change in the way we live.

The hope for a Suffering Servant
Isaiah 53

In Isaiah 53, there is talk about God choosing a servant who would suffer on behalf of all the people. Somehow, the suffering which this servant would go through would benefit all human beings.

This is certainly a different view of hope from the usual one.

If you are looking for a great new king, you are thinking of one who has the power to get rid of enemies and act with strength. How can we be better off if our leader is someone who suffers and even dies? How can that change anything?

Most Jews did not think of Isaiah 53 as a hope for the future. Their hope for a future king was for someone with power, not someone who was beaten. They thought that this chapter in Isaiah was a look at the suffering of Israel and that its purpose was to try to make sense out of that experience rather than to look ahead for a new leader. That is, most Jews thought of the Suffering Servant as the whole people of God who had gone through the exile experience. Somehow all human beings would benefit from what had happened to them.

After Jesus died and rose again, this passage became very important for Christians. The new king was, in fact, one who suffered for his people. He was not a king of this world; those who hoped for that kind of Messiah were disappointed.

The hope for a final victory
Daniel 12:1-13

A final kind of hope that emerges in the Old Testament is the hope that God will one day enter into a battle with everything that is evil and destroy it once and for all. After the final battle takes place, all the faithful ones will be set up to live forever in happiness and peace. We have such visions of the end of things in Daniel.

These are the different kinds of hope that emerged among the prophets during the exile and later. Have they all been fulfilled? Was Jesus the answer to all of these expressions of hope? When we get to the New Testament we shall see that some people were very disappointed in Jesus. He was not what they were hoping for at all.

Others, whose hopes were defined in different ways, were able to say that Jesus was, in fact, the one God had sent to make all things right.

We still live in a world that has to live in hope. Conditions are not perfect; we long for that time of rest and peace and contentment when there is genuine love among all people, and those things begun in Jesus have been completed. We live in the hope that God will continue to keep all his promises.

The Survivors Return

The chance to go home

Ezra 1:1-5

Have you ever had the experience of returning to some place that you had not seen for a long time? Maybe it was a house where you used to live, or some woods or a field where you used to play, or a church or school that you used to attend. Then perhaps your family took a trip and you were able to go back to this place. You were so excited about it that you could hardly wait. But when you got there, something was wrong. It was all so different, not half as pleasant as you remembered it to be. How come?

Maybe you remembered it correctly, but it had changed. Your house had been torn down and replaced by a supermarket, or the woods or meadow was now a subdivision, or the church or school was full of people you didn't know.

Or maybe the problem was simply that you were different. The things that thrilled you when you were 6 years old don't impress you when you are 14, or 20, or 40 years old. Something that looked awfully big to a three-footer doesn't look so big to a six-footer.

You can't go back. If you do go back, it won't be the same. Your memory plays tricks on you. Things have changed in the place that you left. You, too, have changed.

During the years of the exile in Babylon, the Jews dreamed

85

of the day when they could return to their land. They believed that God, faithful to his promise, would some day bring them back to continue their life as a nation. After the period of punishment was over, there would be a glorious return. The prophets encouraged them in this hope.

And the prophets were right. There was a momentous change in world politics that gave the Jews the chance they had been hoping for. About 50 years after the exile began, Babylon was defeated by the Persians. The king of the Persians was Cyrus. The prophet who wrote the second part of the book of Isaiah (beginning with Chapter 40) was so excited about what was happening that he even referred to Cyrus as God's Messiah (that is, *anointed*) in Isa. 45:1.

The Babylonians had tried to control the people they defeated by taking them away from their homes and moving them around to different parts of the empire. The Persians, on the other hand, were much more willing to let people live in their own lands, keep their own customs, and practice their own religion.

Thus, soon after he became king, Cyrus issued an order that the Jews could return to Jerusalem and rebuild their temple. Many of the Jews, who had been longing for a chance to return, did exactly that. The biblical books that tell us about this time are Ezra, Nehemiah, and the prophets Haggai and Zechariah.

It was not a glorious time in the history of God's people. They found they could not go back to the good old days.

So it was not one of those grand times—like the exodus or the time of David and Solomon. Rather, it was a time of hanging on, regrouping, trying to start over. There were some accomplishments. Some hopes were fulfilled. But there were many problems and unfulfilled promises as well. First let us look at some of the accomplishments.

The return home

Some of the Jews did return to their land. This was no small achievement. The hopes of the people of God were bound up in the idea that they should be a nation in a particular place—the land of Palestine which God had promised them. There was no other place on the face of the earth that could substitute for it. There was only one land of Israel and only one city of Jerusalem.

Since the time of the exile, Jews have lived all over the world. Many of them decided to stay in Babylon, even when they had a chance to go back. But it is important even for those Jews who live in other countries that there be a Jewish nation in Palestine. That was the case 500 years before Christ. It is still true today.

Today we know how important it was for God's people to return to their land. For it was in that land, in places like Bethlehem and Nazareth and Jerusalem, that God revealed himself in the life of Jesus.

The temple rebuilt
Haggai 1:1-11; Zechariah 1:7-17

Another success of this period was the rebuilding of the temple and the wall around Jerusalem. The loss of the temple had been one of the most bitter results of the exile. It is hard for us to imagine how important the temple was to the Jew. It was the center of worship and certain ceremonies and sacrifices could take place only in the temple. Some people made such a strong connection between the temple and God that they couldn't imagine worshiping him in any other place.

When the exiles returned, one of the first things they did was to start rebuilding the temple. But things soon bogged down. Morale was low. It was one thing to dream about the new temple in Jerusalem. It was another thing to have to come up with some money, and to sweat and strain doing the work of putting those heavy stones in place. It was demanding work. And the exiles tended to excuse themselves from that job because they had so much to do to get their own houses rebuilt.

Then two prophets came on the scene to give words of encouragement. Haggai told them if they would quit worrying about their own property and get to work on the temple, everything, including the rain and the crops, would improve. Zechariah had a number of visions showing God's determination to restore Jerusalem and the temple. By 515 B.C., the temple was built. Again the Jews had a rallying point, a place to worship their God. This temple had been rebuilt, with some additions, by the time of Jesus.

A little later, when morale again was low and there was danger from enemies, a strong leader named Nehemiah helped them build a wall around the city. This was needed to protect them from hostile neighbors and make their survival possible.

Putting together the Bible
Nehemiah 8:1-8

An important accomplishment during this time was the beginning of the Bible in the form we now have. In the stories of this period we first hear about a collection of writings called the Law of Moses. Ezra, another important leader from this time, had brought this Law with him from Babylon and taught it to the people.

It is a good guess that during the exile Jewish scholars began to collect the ancient stories, poems, prophetic statements, and other material from their past. They wanted to be sure that the record of what had happened between God and his people would not get lost in the destruction and exile.

When Ezra returned to Jerusalem from Babylon, he may have brought with him part of our present Bible—perhaps the first five books, or at least a major portion of them. This would be the beginning of a collection of sacred books that eventually became the Old and New Testaments. Now the people of God

had writings that gave a link between the events of the past and the hopes of the future.

So there were some good things that happened in this period. There were also some problems and unfulfilled promises.

Isolation

Ezra 10:1-5

There was a tendency for God's people to isolate themselves from the rest of the world. They were so concerned with survival, with not losing their identity, with keeping their worship and doctrine pure, that they had no time or energy for their task of mission to the world.

When you are desperately trying to stay alive in the midst of hostile people and difficult conditions, it is almost impossible to feel love and generosity to those outside your own group. An example of this kind of attitude among the Jews is the agreement to give up foreign wives and their children. Mixed marriages were forbidden because they tended to confuse the pure faith.

Some students of the Bible think that the little books of Jonah and Ruth were written at this time. Their purpose was to speak against this narrowness and to remind the Jews that their God is the God of the whole world. These little books reminded them of their mission to be a blessing to all of humanity.

Legalism

Another problem that began to develop was a tendency toward legalism and "bookism." That is, the law is written in a book and that book is studied very carefully to be sure everyone lives exactly as it specifies. There is little room for personal freedom and decision. There is a constant looking backward. The exile was looked at as a result of not keeping the law. In order to be sure that kind of disaster would not happen again, everyone had to be very careful to obey the law perfectly. Then God would never send such punishment again.

This is different from a view that thinks of the law as a guide given by God, but knows that God already loves us before he gives the law. When you start to think of the law as something that has to be obeyed perfectly in order to gain God's favor, you are in deep trouble because no one can do that. Some of that kind of thinking began to develop in this time of return from exile. It was certainly a view among some of the Jews at the time of Jesus.

Disappointment

As we have already noticed, there was certainly disappointment among those who wanted to return to a glorious past. We have seen enough of this history to know there never was very much glory in their past—only a few years here and there. The return was a partial fulfillment of hopes and promises—but hardly enough to satisfy anyone. If their hope was for a strong new king, or a nation that was free and powerful, or a life without hardship and conflict, then it had not happened yet.

Some things had improved. God's people still existed and worshiped and remembered what God had done for them in the past—and hoped. The prophets were still studied. Their descriptions of what God would do in the future were examined carefully. He would certainly do something more for his people. What would it be?

Stories, Songs, and Wisdom

The human response

We are near the end of our Old Testament story. The books of the Old Testament were written by people God had chosen. These descendants of Abraham reflected on what God was doing and what this meant for them. They asked questions about the past and the present, and trusted God to continue his promises in the future.

But before we leave our study of the Old Testament, we should look at several books which are a bit different from those we have looked at so far. In these books, the emphasis is not so much on what God has done, but on our human response to what he has done. That is, the main point is not to tell what God is doing, but to start from the human side—sharing our hopes, dreams, thoughts, and feelings with God.

So, under this general heading of "human response," let us look at three kinds of writing: story, song, and wisdom.

Stories

You may wonder why we have a separate category for *story*. Haven't we been studying stories all along? We have, but in the stories we have been looking at there was an effort to tell the story the way it really happened.

There is another way of telling stories, however, in order to explain some important truth about who God is or what it is like to be a human being in this world. For example, the pastor may tell a story in his sermon in order to help us understand something about God. Or, as we shall see in later chapters, Jesus often told parables about everyday life so his hearers could understand his message better.

Such stories are not necessarily history. They may be based on real people or real events, but are not told in order to describe something that actually happened in the past. Their main purpose is to answer religious questions.

There are stories like that in the Old Testament. One example is the story of Ruth, a foreign woman who became the great grandmother of David. Another example is the story of Jonah, the reluctant prophet whom God used to reach the Assyrians, even against Jonah's own wishes. Both stories show concern for people outside Israel and counteract tendencies toward exclusiveness. Another story is the Book of Esther, the beautiful woman who saved her people from persecution by the Persians. This explains the origin of the Feast of Purim.

There is disagreement over these stories. Some people insist they must be treated as actual happenings. Others claim they are stories, or parables, with the main emphasis being on their message. Either way, they have value for us.

Songs

Psalm 150; Psalm 22; Song of Solomon 2:8-17

The book of Psalms is the longest book in the Bible. It is a collection of 150 separate psalms used for worship by God's people and often still used in worship today.

There are many different kinds of psalms. Some of them are hymns of praise, focusing our attention on God and the wonderful things he has done. A frequent refrain in the psalms is, "O give thanks to the Lord, for he is good, for his steadfast love endures for ever." There are several psalms of this type at the end of the book, such as Psalm 150, which concludes, "Let everything that breathes praise the Lord! Praise the Lord!"

Some psalms are thanksgiving songs. One of the best examples of such a psalm is not even in the book of Psalms but is in Jonah 2:1-9. Thanksgiving psalms may have been used in a ser-

vice of thanksgiving after deliverance from some danger which had threatened the community or nation.

A number of psalms are associated with the king. Some may have been used at a coronation. Psalm 45 has to do with a royal wedding. These psalms speak of God's support for the king, whom he calls his son, as in Ps. 2:7. By the end of the Old Testament times, these psalms had come to be regarded as "messianic" psalms. That is, they were studied carefully by those who were hoping for a new Messiah, a new king, to sit on David's throne. Some of them are referred to in the New Testament. An example is Ps. 110:1, "The Lord says to my lord: 'Sit at my right hand, till I make your enemies your footstool'" (see also Matt. 22:44).

The largest group of songs is the laments and Psalm 22 is a good example. We have already seen other laments in the books of Jeremiah and Lamentations. It seems to have been appropriate for an individual or group or the whole nation to bring their pains, anxieties, and despair before the congregation. They knew they would get no relief from inner turmoil by holding it all in and pretending that everything was all right.

We Christians do not make much use of these laments. They are full of complaints and griping, and at times the writer even argues with God. Somehow today we have the notion that you are not supposed to talk like that, so we are very careful to make our prayers sound nice and respectful—as if we could fool God by our good manners.

But the laments apparently had a very helpful effect on those who used them. As you read through Psalm 22, you will notice a gradual improvement in the mood. Maybe just talking it out in the supporting atmosphere of community worship was enough. Maybe some official of the temple said a word of hope from God at some point during the psalm. At any rate, this psalm, like many laments, ends on an upbeat.

Jesus used laments on at least one occasion. One of his last words from the cross is the opening line of Psalm 22: "My God, my God, why hast thou forsaken me?"

Another kind of song is found in the Song of Solomon, or Song of Songs. It is a lovely collection of songs and poems about human love, supposedly written by Solomon. He had a reputation as a wise man. In 1 Kings 4:32 the Bible says he was the author of 3000 proverbs and 1,005 songs. He was also the husband of 1000 women, which may or may not have qualified him to write songs about love.

There are many different opinions about how to understand the Song of Songs. If they really are what they seem to be, songs of love between a man and a woman, then it is hard for many to understand why they are in the Bible. They are not directly religious. They do not talk about God and his relations with his people.

The most common understanding of this collection of songs has been to think of it as an allegory, that is, a kind of story used to express a truth about the love of God for his people. In an allegory, everything stands for something other than what it seems to. In these songs, the man really represents God, and the woman represents God's people. Jesus and the prophets often said that the love of God is like that of a husband for his wife. So what looks like simple love poetry is really telling us something about God after all.

Another way to think about these songs is to take them for what they seem to be. Then this book becomes a strong statement about how God puts his blessing on human love, the good creation that he made, and on the sexual attraction between men and women. We are not to be ashamed of our human bodies or the love that we feel and wish to express to some special person of the opposite sex.

So we can read this little book in either of these two ways, or both. In any case, there is a meaningful message for us, and the many kinds of writing that are in the Bible continue to surprise us.

Wisdom
Proverbs 15; Ecclesiastes 1:1-11; 3:1-9

There are other parts of the Old Testament that are called wisdom literature. This material represents the efforts of human beings to use their minds in order to understand their world. Wisdom comes from people reflecting on their experiences.

One of the things that God gave us in creation is the ability to use our minds. This ability is something that sets us apart from any other creature God made. God intends us to use our minds. We are not to fear that if we think and raise questions, we are in danger of losing our faith. A faith that never raises any questions is probably a faith that hasn't looked very closely at the world.

There are two main kinds of wisdom. The first is represented by most of the book of Proverbs. It is a collection of common-sense sayings about life from a wise person who has observed life carefully.

There is another kind of wisdom which moves a step beyond such helpful hints to good living. It, too, is based on personal reflection on human experience, but recognizes the disappointments in life. Sometimes the good people suffer and the bad live to a happy old age in wealth and security. Sometimes it is hard to see that the world makes the kind of sense that Proverbs says it does.

Two examples of this second kind of wisdom are Job and Ecclesiastes. Job is the story of a good man who suffers, and of his search to find a satisfactory explanation from God as to why it should happen to him. He got no help from friends who tried to counsel him. Finally, God himself gave him an answer which was not really an answer. That is, there is no simple explanation for all bad things in the world, but God does care and does come to us in our despair.

Ecclesiastes is a strange little book; many wish it were not in the Bible. It, too, was supposedly written by the wise Solomon. It is a book that appeals to many modern people because of its pessimistic mood. "Nothing makes sense. You might as well find what enjoyment you can in this life because death is the great equalizer and there is nothing left when we are gone."

Ecclesiastes, especially, shows us a human reaction to what life is all about. It is certainly not the whole answer. But it is a legitimate human response, and it is honored by being preserved in the Bible.

In all these examples of human response, there is complete honesty before God. If you feel like the writer of Ecclesiastes, then it is okay to say so. You don't have to pretend that you feel like singing a hymn of praise. You cannot fool God or hide anything from him. Tell him the way it is with you, and he will come to you to help, no matter where you are.

The Time Between

A dark age

There are times in human history that have been called *dark ages*. This could mean that they were bad times in which to live. Or it could mean they were dark in the sense that we don't know much about them. The period between the end of the Old Testament and the beginning of the New Testament is a *dark age* in both ways.

After the stories of Ezra and Nehemiah, the Old Testament is a complete blank as far as telling us what was going on. There are a few Old Testament books, or parts of books, that come from this time, but they are not historical accounts. Rather, they are poetry or wisdom or psalms or something called apocalyptic. The last Old Testament book to be written was probably Daniel; it is an example of what is called apocalyptic.

Our information concerning this period from about 350 B.C. to the time of Jesus Christ comes from sources outside the Bible. The books of the Maccabees (which are part of the Roman Catholic Bible but not the Protestant Bible) and the writing of Josephus (a Jewish historian at the end of the first century A.D.) are especially valuable. We have also learned much about this period through the findings of archaeologists, particularly from the caves of the community of Qumran near the Dead Sea. It was a time of unfulfilled hopes and some very difficult trials. It was a time of almost endless political tyranny, with some deliverance, and then back to tyranny again. Let's look at some of the happenings of this period.

Greek influence

Alexander the Great was the new world conqueror. This meant the Jews were under the control of Greeks rather than Persians. Like the Persians, the Greeks allowed defeated people a considerable amount of freedom to run their own affairs, so it probably wasn't too bad for those who lived under their control.

Greek influence was felt in all parts of that world. For example, Greek became the common language. After a few generations of this, most Jews couldn't speak Hebrew anymore, especially Jews who lived in places like the city of Alexandria in Egypt. How could you study the Hebrew Bible if you didn't know Hebrew? So sometime around 250 B.C., scholars began translating the Old Testament into Greek. The Greek Old Testament, known as the Septuagint, was the Bible of most of the early Christians, who were much more at home in Greek than in Hebrew, and the New Testament was written in Greek.

Some of the Jews who were learning about Greek philosophy, architecture, medicine, literature, and athletics were very impressed with Greek culture. They wanted to borrow some of these things and fit them in with their own religion. Other Jews were opposed to this. Like Ezra, they insisted their religion was unique and could not be combined with foreign ways of thinking without losing its heart.

This conflict between the old ways and the new Greek ideas continued for some time and was still going on among the followers of Jesus after his resurrection. In other ways it is still going on in our own day when we struggle to hold on to the old ideas while making them fit the modern world.

Guerrilla warfare

When Alexander the Great died, his kingdom was split into several parts. For a long time, Palestine was controlled by Egypt. But after 200 B.C., the control shifted to Syria. There began to be less and less freedom for the Jews to run their own government and worship in their own way.

One of the Syrian kings, Antiochus Epiphanes, ruled from 175 to 164 B.C. He forced the Jews to do things their religion condemned. They had to make the choice between obeying the Hebrew law and being a traitor to the state, or obeying the king

and violating the commandments of God. The crowning blow came when Antiochus sacrificed a pig on the altar of the temple. Now good Jews felt it was impossible to worship in the temple anymore.

The Jews began to organize to fight back. A family of priests were the leaders in this rebellion, the most famous of them being Judas Maccabaeus. Their guerrilla warfare was very effective. The temple was restored, purified, and rededicated. The Jewish festival of Hanukkah still celebrates this event today. The Greek rulers were forced to give up some of their control, and for about 100 years Judea was ruled by members of the priestly family that had led the rebellion.

We know something about this period from the books of the Maccabees, which are part of what is called the Apocrypha. The Apocrypha contains books that were written during this time between the two Testaments. Unlike the Old Testament books, they were never accepted by the Jews as part of Holy Scripture. Protestants have followed the Jews here, accepting them as helpful books, but not on the same level as the rest of the Bible.

Courage from Daniel

Daniel 7:1-14; 12:1-13

The last book of the Old Testament to be written was probably Daniel. Most scholars believe that it was written during the persecution of Antiochus Epiphanes in order to give moral support to those who were suffering for what they believed. It tells the story of an ancient hero, Daniel, who also suffered for what he believed. But God delivered Daniel from all sorts of dangers, even the lions' den. The readers of the book of Daniel were to take courage from that example.

The last half of Daniel is a series of visions describing the end of the world. This is an example of a kind of literature known as apocalyptic. An example of apocalyptic literature in the New Testament is the book of Revelation. This kind of writing comes out of times of great trouble when it looks as if there is little hope.

Apocalyptic writing recognizes that the world is in such bad shape that God himself is going to have to go to war against the powers of evil. It talks about how the end of the world is coming soon. The description of how this will happen is full of images of strange beasts. It is a code language. Those who heard or read it at the time knew that the lion was Babylon, the bear was the Medes, the leopard the Persians, and the dragon the Greeks. Those of us reading this in later centuries have not always known who these beasts were.

At different times in history, people have thought the world was coming to an end and have looked back at apocalyptic books like Daniel and tried to connect those strange creatures with powerful nations in their own day. So far, the world has not ended. When will it happen? So far, everyone who has made predictions has been wrong. The best answer was given by Jesus to his followers just before he left them: "It is not for you to know times or seasons which the Father has fixed by his own authority" (Acts 1:6-7).

One other thing which emerges clearly in the book of Daniel is a belief in the resurrection of the dead. Earlier parts of the Old Testament are not clear about life after death.

Daniel says to stand firm in your faith. Even if you must suffer death, do not be afraid. God will be with you as he was with Daniel. In fact, the end of the world is coming soon. God will destroy the enemy and put the Son of man in charge. All who have died for his cause will come back to life and live in everlasting peace. Those who have been unfaithful will be brought back to life for everlasting shame and contempt.

An evil king

After the successful rebellion, the Jews had another chance to rule themselves. It didn't work. The 100-year reign of the Jewish priest-princes was a time of corruption, plotting for power, and oppression of the people. So there was no improvement, only more disappointed hopes.

Then from about 63 B.C., Judea was under the influence of Rome. The evil king Herod the Great ruled for about 30 years and died in 4 B.C. He was the kind of king who would do anything to get and keep power, and he knew how to please the Romans in order to do this. He murdered anyone who seemed to be a threat, including the last survivors of the priestly rulers and even members of his own family. Like the pharaoh of

Moses' time, he condemned the male babies of Bethlehem to be killed. But Jesus, like Moses, was saved from that fate.

How to survive?

There was considerable disagreement among the Jews as to how to survive in such a world. What were they to think and do? Where was God in all this? Many lost confidence in the possibility of ever having a decent leader. Some people became professional compromisers. "If you can't beat them, join them. Make the best deal you can. Play the game in order to get as much for yourself as possible."

Others tried to remove themselves from all the worldly conflict. They tried to survive in a hostile society, keep the law, and wait for God to do something. If they were pure and obedient to God's word, they would be on the right side when God finally decided to take action against the evil ones.

Others went a step further and actually packed up and moved out of the towns and cities and formed communes. These were places where they could live together with others who had the same desire to keep themselves unspoiled by the world. They expected the end of the world to come soon and planned to be ready. The Essenes who collected the Dead Sea Scrolls were such a group.

A variation of this approach was to expect a mighty battle at the end of the world, and to be prepared to participate in that battle for God in a great holy war. The problem was knowing when to pick up arms and start to fight.

Still another reaction to the disillusionment of the times was to become a "freedom fighter." The one most important thing to do was to get rid of Roman authority. Having accomplished that, a new government could be set up, possibly with a king from the family of David.

This was the world into which Jesus was born. These many expectations, hopes, and disappointments were in the background of his thinking and also influenced the way his followers understood him and told the story about him.

At this point in time, God's people did not really know what they needed. But they certainly needed something. As he had done in the past, God saw their need. He knew what to do. He sent a new kind of king: his Son, Jesus.

The Old Testament Period

	Biblical era	Leaders	Prophets	World powers
2000 B.C.				
	Patriarchs	Abraham Isaac Jacob Joseph		
1300				
	Exodus	Moses Aaron		E g y p t A s s y r i a
1200		Joshua		
	Judges	Ehud Jephthah		
1100		Deborah Gideon		
		Samson	Samuel	
1000	United Kingdom (1020-922)	Saul David Solomon	Nathan	
900	Divided Kingdom (922-722)	11 kings in Judah	Elijah Elisha	Syria
800		19 kings in Israel	Amos Hosea Isaiah Micah	Assyria
700	Judah alone (722-587)	9 kings including Josiah	Zephaniah Nahum Jeremiah Habbakuk	Babylon
600				
500	Exile and return	Nehemiah Ezra	Ezekiel Obadiah Haggai Joel Zechariah Malachi	Persia
400	Inter- testamental period	Maccabees	Daniel	Greece
100				Jewish independence
A.D.				Rome

Time Line

B.C.		
2000		
1900		
1800		**Patriarchs**
		Abraham
1700		Isaac
		Jacob
1600		Joseph
1500		
1400		
1300		**Exodus from Egypt**
1200		**Conquest**
1100		**Period of the judges**
1000		**United monarchy**
		Saul, David, Solomon
900		Solomon dies 922
		Israel and Judah 922-722
800		Elijah about 850
		First writing prophets after 750
700		**Kingdom of Judah** 722-587
		Jerusalem falls 587
600		
		Babylonian exile
500		
		Resettlement under Persian rule
400		Rebuilding of temple
300		**Intertestamental period**
		Maccabean revolt 168
200		
100		**Roman supremacy**
		BIRTH OF CHRIST
		Jerusalem destroyed 70
A.D. 100		

The Story of God's Love
Part 2

The story continues

The story of God's love for people like you and me is a long
one. After 39 books in the Old Testament and a few thousand
years of Abraham, Isaac, Jacob, Moses, David, and all of the
children of Israel, you have only heard half of it.

It has been a great story so far, a story about people who are
chosen by God to be his special nation in the world. People
who are honest and good and trustworthy. People who are
cheaters, liars, and murderers. Lots of people who are both good
and bad. Remember the terrible famine and the brothers who
sold their little brother Joseph to slave traders and then later
had to ask him for help? Then there was the time when God
sent Moses to lead his people out of slavery and when God
rescued all of them from the Egyptians by a miracle at the sea.
And do you recall the bloody war fought to get a homeland for
the people?

There have been some great leaders and judges and kings,
and there have been some miserable failures. Israel didn't always win the wars. Once they were dragged off to Babylonia
and lived as slaves for several generations before God brought
them back to their homeland again. Page after page, the story
has been full of people. Powerful people, prophets, kings, and
priests. Poor people, kids, sick people, and mean people.

God likes people. That is what the story has really been saying. In fact, God loves people, all sorts of people—even people

like you—indeed *you*. God has chosen *you* to be one of his special people. That is the point of the story.

The best part of the story is still to come. If you have started to catch on that this is really a story about God and you, then you are on the right track. The story of God's love for you and me is an amazing one.

A library

The Old Testament has 39 books and the New Testament has 27. So the Bible is not just a book. It is a library. It is the book of books, and this book is full of an amazing assortment of stories, letters, poems, prayers, and prophecies.

Among the 27 New Testament books are four that tell the story of Jesus. These are the gospels: Matthew, Mark, Luke, and John. Though similar in many ways, they also differ in what they say about Jesus.

Then there is the book called The Acts of the Apostles. It tells the story of the words and deeds of Jesus' followers or disciples after he was gone. Next come 21 books which are mostly letters from some of the first Christians, like the apostle Paul, who wrote to individuals and congregations they had come to know.

And finally, the last book in the Bible is The Revelation to John. It is a book about the end or the last things in the world. So our long story does have an end.

Where should we begin?

Where were we when we finished the Old Testament? Why not just pick up where we left off with the people looking for God to rescue them once again and set up his kingdom? Why not just talk about what Jesus said and did and how he was the Savior God sent to his people?

Why not? Because there was a problem. Most of the people in Jesus' country did not believe that he was the leader God had sent to save them. They had other ideas of how God should do it. Some of them wanted a great king like David or a military leader like Joshua. Some were expecting a prophet like Moses or Elijah who would lead a big religious revival. Some people were hoping for a new high priest for the temple, and many others felt things were so bad that God would destroy the world and only a few faithful people would be saved for a fresh start.

All of these different groups read the Old Testament carefully. In fact, they thought they had it all figured out—in the same way that some people today think they have it all figured out. God himself couldn't change their minds!

That was the problem!

But the followers of Jesus also read the Old Testament carefully. And they believed that Jesus really was the one God had sent to save the world. After Easter, they were convinced of it!

So, they told everybody about Jesus. They worked hard to show that what Jesus said and did was part of the long story of the Old Testament. They were out to show that Jesus was exactly the kind of Savior that God—the God of the Old Testament—would send.

At first they just told the story, one person to another or a few believers to their Jewish relatives and friends. Before long there were a great number of people telling the story about Jesus, sometimes even to persons who hadn't heard the story of the Old Testament before. Eventually there were some people who got the story all confused and missed the point.

Thus the day came when some Christian leaders began to write down parts of the story and their explanations of it. They wanted to be sure the true message of Christ was available for everyone. First it was people like Paul writing letters to churches and people who needed to be straightened out or who needed encouragement. Generally these letters just reminded the people of what they had been told. But later the most important parts of the story about Jesus were also written down. Probably about 35 to 60 years after Jesus' life on earth, the four gospel writers or evangelists each told the story once again, this time in writing.

The timeline was probably about like this:

ministry of Jesus	the story of Jesus is told	Paul writes his letters	the four gospels are written	the book of Revelation is written

A.D. 27-30   50   65   90 100

The gospels tell the story

The gospels were probably written after many of the other books in the New Testament, but we begin with them because they show us how Jesus fits in the long story that we have been following in the Old Testament. The gospels do not tell us everything we might like to know about Jesus. As the ending of The Gospel According to John says, "But there are also many other things which Jesus did; were every one of them to be written, I suppose the world itself could not contain the books that would be written." [1]

But the gospels do tell us what the disciples and followers of Jesus believed was most important. After people had been telling about Jesus for several years, these writers or evangelists saved the stories that showed most clearly that Jesus is the one God sent to save the world. They put these accounts together in the gospels.

The four gospel writers do not all tell us exactly the same things. Sometimes Matthew, Mark, and Luke agree almost word for word; and since Luke tells us that he knew about other Christian books,[2] it seems that Luke and Matthew copied parts of their gospels from Mark. But each evangelist also tells us stories about Jesus that none of the others tell, and often one of the gospels will even change what is in another gospel.

Remember, God's message was written and told by people. Each person was speaking or writing to other people. You wouldn't use the same words to tell a first grader about a championship game as you would to describe it to a big league player. But it is still the same ball game. You just want to make sure that both of them realize how important and exciting the game was!

And that is what each of the gospel writers wanted to do. He knew a great many stories about what Jesus said and did in his years on earth. He knew that all of this is really one very long story with an amazing and wonderful conclusion. And he was eager to tell the whole story to his friends and family and all people, including *you*.

The story is true. It started back with Abraham—even way before Abraham. It is God's story. It is the story of his love for all his creation. And Jesus is the center of the story!

1. John 21:25
2. Luke 1:1

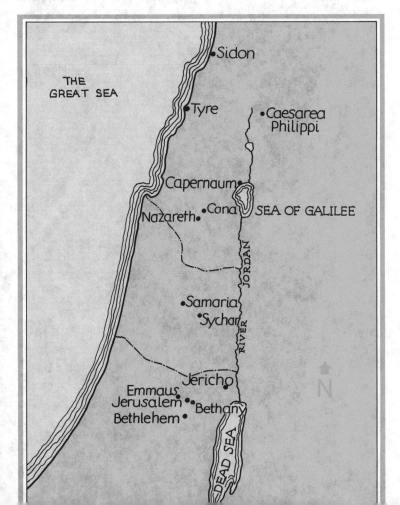

Death to King Jesus!

Luke 22:14—23:56

A matter of life and death

Let's face it: You are going to die. So am I. There is no use kidding ourselves. One day the pastor will gather your friends and family around your grave and read, "Ashes to ashes and dust to dust." Maybe you will live to be 101. Maybe you won't. One way or another, your life will end in death. Nobody ever gets out alive.

Now, that may sound grim, but it is the truth. Maybe you have already experienced the death of a friend or a relative, a grandparent, or maybe even your mom or dad. Perhaps you have actually come close to dying yourself. But at least you know by now that one day, sooner or later, you are going to die.

It just doesn't seem right! It's a bad deal!

Back in Genesis 3 the people of God knew that death was part of what was wrong about this world. Death is proof that sin and evil and the power of destruction are real, as real as the jealousy and cruelty that we often show each other.

So why doesn't God do something? Why doesn't he just destroy all the evil people, as he did with a flood in Noah's day or with fire and brimstone as he did to Sodom and Gomorrah? Or better yet, why doesn't he try to save the world? You know, send some prophets or messengers to tell us how to live. Or he could even come himself to get rid of sin and evil and death.

111

Why doesn't God just set up his own government and make the world like the Garden of Eden again?

The point of our whole story is that God has done something. He is still at work today. He wants us to live, not die. He wants to save us, not destroy us.

But what about death and what about evil? What has God done about them?

Crucify him! Crucify him!

The gospels and Paul's letters emphasize that the death of Jesus is the center of the whole story. If you read Chapters 6-8 of Paul's letter to the Romans and Chapter 15 of his first letter to the Corinthians, you will see that the death of Jesus was God's answer to the sin, evil, and death that are so real in our lives.

We pick up the story in Luke 22. Jesus was having his last supper with his disciples. He talked about suffering and betrayal and death. As Luke tells the story, Jesus and his friends were celebrating the Passover. It was a yearly celebration when Jews remembered how God rescued his Chosen People from slavery in Egypt. But this time it looked as if Jesus was going to be the Passover lamb himself. His body and blood would be sacrificed.

Jesus' disciples couldn't make any sense out of it at the time. Instead they had visions of the glory of the kingdom and of the important positions they would get. They were not even ready to remain awake while Jesus prayed in the darkness, struggling with the threat of death. The disciples were unprepared for the fact that they themselves would betray and desert Jesus.

So when Jesus was arrested and executed, nobody knew what to say or do. Everyone felt terrible, as is often the case with a tragic death. It seemed as if injustice, evil, and death had won. Nothing Jesus had said or done, his message of God's love, his healing of the sick and lame and blind, his devotion to his friends—none of it made any difference to them. Only the haunting question remained, "Where is God?"

The record is clear: Jesus died an ugly, humiliating death. There is no getting around it. The four gospel writers all tell about that death in their own ways. Mark stresses the terror of Jesus crying out, "My God, my God, why hast thou forsaken me?" [1] Matthew makes it sound like the beginning of the end of the world, complete with earthquakes and dead bodies coming out of tombs.[2] John emphasizes the fact that Jesus was executed for being "The King of the Jews."[3] All the gospels tell about Jesus' death in great detail, and all are asking, "Would God allow this to happen to the king of his Chosen People?"

The gospels force us to face the strange twist of the story. This "Chosen One" was arrested in the dark of the night like a common crook and was crucified along with two criminals. This Messiah was rejected by the leaders of the people he came to save, and those leaders scoffed at him while he was hanging on the cross, saying, "He saved others; let him save himself, if he is the Christ of God, his Chosen One!" This king was charged with encouraging rebellion against the government and executed with a sign above his head that read, "This is the King of the Jews." He was roughed up by a dishonest king named Herod, and finally he was sentenced to die by a Roman official named Pilate who let the mob decide.

It certainly looked as if God were not in control!

Only later—after the resurrection—did it begin to make sense. By the time the Gospels were written, Jesus' followers had seen the light of Easter morning and had gone back to study the Scriptures once again. Then the pieces began to fit.

Yes, Jesus was "The King of the Jews, the Christ of God, his Chosen One." God had sent his Son to be a new kind of king, reigning with love and forgiveness.

But the majesty and power of this king and his kingdom were not obvious to people who expected kings to have great riches and huge armies. The crowd rejected God's king. They thought his words of forgiveness and his acceptance of death were just signs of weakness. They did not recognize the strength of God at work. Instead they shouted, "Crucify him! Crucify him!" and they sneered at him as he died.

But all along, God was working a miracle. In the midst of the gloom of Good Friday, the God who called Abraham and spoke to Moses and inspired the prophets was involved. All the clues to his presence were scattered around so that someone who knew the Scriptures could find them. And once God had finished the miracle on Easter morning, Jesus' followers could finally understand. When the world had done its worst, God had done his best. He gave love and forgiveness to all humanity.

Despised and rejected

Isa. 53:1-12 is the Old Testament background that gave the disciple Philip the chance to tell an official from Ethiopia the good news of Jesus.[4] Somehow that old prophecy was just the right word, particularly in the opinion of the writer of Luke and Acts. The death of Jesus began to make sense. The pieces fit.

Isaiah 53	Luke 22-23
He was despised and rejected by men; a man of sorrows, and acquainted with grief; and as one from whom men hide their faces he was despised, and we esteemed him not.	For the Son of man goes as it has been determined; but woe to that man by whom he is betrayed!" And they began to question one another, which of them it was that would do this.
	And he said to him, "Lord, I am ready to go with you to prison and to death." He said, I tell you, Peter, the cock will not crow this day, until you three times deny that you know me."
	And when he rose from prayer, he came to the disciples and found them sleeping for sorrow, and he said to them, "Why do you sleep? Rise and pray that you may not enter into temptation."
	While he was still speaking, there came a crowd, and the man called Judas, one of the twelve, was leading them. He drew near to Jesus to kiss him: but Jesus said to him, "Judas, would you betray the Son of man with a kiss?"
Surely he has borne our griefs and carried our sorrows; yet we esteemed him stricken, smitten by God, and afflicted. But he was wounded for our transgressions, he was bruised for our iniquities;	Now the men who were holding Jesus mocked him and beat him; they also blindfolded him and asked him, "Prophesy! Who is it that struck you?" And they spoke many other words against him, reviling him.

upon him was the chastisement that made us whole,
and with his stripes we are healed.

The chief priests and the scribes stood by, vehemently accusing him. And Herod with his soldiers treated him with contempt and mocked him; then, arraying him in gorgeous apparel, he sent him back to Pilate.

"I will therefore chastise him and release him."

But they shouted out, "Crucify, crucify him!" A third time he said to them, "Why, what evil has he done? I have found in him no crime deserving death; I will therefore chastise him and release him."

He was oppressed, and he was afflicted,
yet he opened not his mouth;
like a lamb that is led to the slaughter,
and like a sheep that before its shearers is dumb,
so he opened not his mouth.

So he questioned him at some length; but he made no answer.

And they made his grave with the wicked
and with a rich man in his death, although he had done no violence, and there was no deceit in his mouth.

Now when the centurion saw what had taken place, he praised God, and said, "Certainly this man was innocent!"

Now there was a man named Joseph from the Jewish town of Arimathea. He was a member of the council, a good and righteous man, who had not consented to their purpose and deed, and he was looking for the kingdom of God. This man went to Pilate and asked for the body of Jesus. Then he took it down and wrapped it in a linen shroud, and laid him in a rock-hewn tomb, where no one had ever yet been laid.

He poured out his soul to death,
and was numbered with the transgressors;
yet he bore the sin of many,
and made intercession for the transgressors.

Two others also, who were criminals, were led away to be put to death with him. And when they came to the place which is called The Skull, there they crucified him, and the criminals, one on the right and one on the left. And Jesus said, "Father, forgive them; for they know not what they do." And they cast lots to divide his garments.

And he said, "Jesus, remember me when you come into your kingdom." And he said to him, "Truly, I say to you, today you will be with me in Paradise."

Then Jesus, crying with a loud voice, said, "Father, into thy hands I commit my spirit!" And having said this he breathed his last.

In the hour of Jesus' death, God was at work. God had not left him in the lurch, although everyone felt he had. Even in his death, in fact especially in his death, Jesus was God's Chosen One, God's suffering servant, doing exactly what God had in mind all along. At last, Jesus' disciples could get the picture. The words of Isaiah said it well: "All we like sheep have gone astray; we have turned every one to his own way; and the Lord has laid on him the iniquity of us all." [5]

The last enemy

God does not ignore our sin or, to use Isaiah's word, our iniquity. He does not let us wander off like straying sheep to our own destruction either. Instead God fights sin and death on its own ground. He sent his Son to take the worst that this sinful, death-dealing world could hand out. So who really is in charge, God or death?

Of course you and I know that we still live in a world where people die. And at funerals it is very hard to make much sense out of death or life. It looks as if death has the last word forever.

But . . . what if God has already proved that the enemy death does not have the last word?[6] What if God is at work even in the suffering and sorrow of death? What if God can turn sorrow to joy and death to life? What if God chose Jesus not only to suffer death but to defeat it? You have to admit, that would be good news!

1. Mark 15:34
2. Matt. 27:51-54
3. John 19:17-22
4. Acts 8:26-40
5. Isa. 53:6
6. 1 Cor. 15:26

Long Live King Jesus!

Luke 24:1-53

He is alive!

Dead bodies stay where they are put. No matter what the horror movies say, corpses don't move. A day, a week, 10 years, a century after the funeral, what's left of a body will still be in the graveyard where it was last buried. People can go there on Memorial Day to plant flowers or say prayers, but nothing really changes in cemeteries.

Yet, once in the gray light of early dawn, some women slipped quietly into a graveyard. Their mission was dangerous. They came to give a proper burial to a man who had been executed as an enemy of the government. Watch out! Don't let anyone catch you befriending such a person, alive or dead.

Yet they stole softly onward. In the chilling silence before daybreak, they found their way among the dark shadows. They knew where the body was, and they braved the dim gloom of the garden, eager to finish their task of embalming it. They hoped they would be gone before anyone spotted them.

They were totally unprepared for what they found. The tomb was empty. The body was gone. What were they going to do?

Suddenly, "two men stood by them in dazzling apparel." Ghosts? Spirits? Angels? "They were frightened." Imagine how you would have felt. Most of us would have gone charging out of that graveyard!

But these "men" had a message. They were angels or messengers of God and their word was, "Why do you seek the living among the dead? Remember how he told you, while he was still in Galilee, that the Son of man must be delivered into the hands of sinful men, and be crucified, and on the third day rise."

Aha! They *did* remember! Those strange words never meant much before. Jesus' disciples had never accepted the idea that he would actually die. So they also forgot about his rising. "Why seek the living among the dead?" Indeed, why? Then they began to realize what had happened. All their hopes and dreams had not been swallowed up by the grave. They rushed out to tell the good news to their friends and the rest of the world.

He broke bread with them

What is a resurrected person like? Have you ever wondered about that? In the life that God gives to his people after death, what will we be like? Will we have fingers and toes or just be a spirit, sort of like a breeze moving from place to place? Who knows?

Well, nobody knows exactly. The closest we come to knowing is the description the gospels give of the resurrected Jesus. And frankly, it is clear that the gospel writers are hard pressed to tell us exactly what Jesus was like after he was raised.

They all agree that the tomb was empty. The body was gone. Luke and John go to some lengths to assure us that Jesus did not just become a ghost with no body. No, his disciples touched him. They even felt the wounds from his execution,[1] and he ate with them.[2]

On the other hand, Jesus appeared and disappeared like a vision. He showed up among them when the doors were shut,[3] and he vanished from their sight. It was the same Jesus, all right, but something had changed. In fact, everything had changed.

At first the disciples did not believe the women who returned from the tomb. The news was too strange. Even the two who walked with Jesus on the road to Emmaus didn't know who he was: "Their eyes were kept from recognizing him." They were deeply moved when he interpreted all the Scriptures beginning with Moses and the prophets, but he was still a mystery to them. Only when he prayed and broke bread with them were their eyes opened. In that meal they saw that the same Jesus who interpreted the Scriptures, prayed, and ate with them before his death was alive and with them once again.

King of all creation

"If Jesus is alive, where is he? Why doesn't he get back to the work of healing the sick and teaching about God? Why isn't he still around and among us? Why did he leave?"

He left because he had finished his mission. He had told us of the God who loves and forgives and cares for his people, the God of Abraham, Isaac, and Jacob. He had also shown that God is in charge, that the ugly power of sin is not as mighty as God. Jesus had walked into the jaws of cruel death, and God raised him from death.

The powerful forces of evil had said that Jesus was not a real king and killed him in an effort to prove it. But God declared Jesus to be the king, the Messiah. He was the only begotten Son who would reign over heaven and earth. Little Palestine, the Roman Empire—the world was too small for him! King Jesus was given charge of all the galaxies and worlds of the whole creation.

Of course, the disciples were slow to understand. Who wouldn't have been? It was all so new, so unbelievable. But when they searched the Scriptures, they began to see that this was exactly what God had in mind since the beginning. Jesus was the key to God's plan to rescue the world he created.

The promise of the Spirit

We are glad to know that God raised Jesus and put him in charge of his kingdom. And it is really important to know that death is not the end, but that God has the final word. Yet what about now? What difference does all this make for your life and mine? What should we do now?

Our job has just begun. As Luke tells us, Jesus has gone. But in the short time between his resurrection and departure, he interpreted the Scriptures, ate with his disciples, and prepared them to go to all nations telling of repentance and forgiveness. And he did not leave them alone, but he sent his Spirit to give them the power to carry out their mission.

In one way, Jesus the Messiah has already done it all. He

has brought God's call for people to change the way they were living. He has told people that God forgives them. He has even faced death so God could show his people once and for all who is really in charge. And he has sent his Spirit to remain with his followers by means of the Scriptures, Baptism, and his Supper. This king, Jesus Christ, has taken care of everything!

Yet in another way, Jesus was just the beginning of the work that God continues to do among his people. Sorrow, pain, sickness, sin, and death still stalk this earth. Everyone has to struggle with them, and many people get discouraged and are ready to give up.

By the time the evangelists had written their accounts of Jesus' life, death, and resurrection, they knew that the long story of God and his people was far from over. This world was not heaven on earth, and it still didn't look much like Eden.

But the turning point in the story had been passed. When the women left the graveyard and when the disciples recognized the risen Jesus, God had already determined how the story would end. He had taken charge, once and for all, in a world where sin and death seemed to reign supreme.

And the gospel writers also knew that God had not abandoned his people. The same Spirit that had been with Jesus, "the promise of my Father" had been sent to help and care for his people until the day when sickness, sin, and death are completely eliminated.

In the meantime, all of us who know the story of God and his people have a job to do. With power from the Holy Spirit we can pass the word: "Don't give up hope. Don't give in to the cruelty and dishonesty and greed and sin around you. God is in charge. King Jesus is for real. God has kept his promises. His kingdom is forever."

No matter what our lives might be like, we know that God's kingdom is real among us in the Scriptures, prayer, Holy Communion, Baptism, and in acts of loving-kindness. God's Spirit is still at work among us. And one day God will completely destroy sin, sickness, and death, just as surely as he raised Jesus from the dead.

"Long live King Jesus!"

---

1. John 20:20-28   3. John 20:19, 26
2. John 21:9-14

Get Ready for the Kingdom

Luke 3 and 4

Remember

When Jesus was gone from the earth, his disciples and friends had work to do. They had been sent out by King Jesus to tell the whole world about his kingdom. The Holy Spirit soon came to enable them to carry on that mission. But that is another part of the story which will be told later.

Right now, try to imagine what it was like for Jesus' friends and disciples once he was gone. How were they supposed to know what to do and when to do it? They could have been like a football team that had lost its head coach. They might well have been in a real mess, with everyone running into each other all over the field.

And the truth is that over the years the followers of Jesus have made a great many mistakes. It is obvious that many Christians say and do things that are just the opposite of what Jesus wants. Sometimes they mean well and still do wrong.

The early disciples made their mistakes, too, but they had a pretty solid idea of what Jesus was about and what he expected of his followers. He had already begun to make them into a team before he left. They had listened to him preach and watched him heal. They had even done some preaching and praying and caring for the poor while he was still with them. So they were ready to carry on with the guidance of his Spirit.

In the first place, they knew it was important to tell everyone about King Jesus. "Jesus is Lord," they said. He is God's Messiah. He is in charge of heaven and earth. Everything they could remember about him that helped make this clear must be told. So beginning with his resurrection, they thought back to the things he said and did. In particular, they were eager to show how the story of Jesus fit with the longer story of God and his people told in our Old Testament.

Secondly, they knew that a disciple should try to be like the teacher and follow the way he led. Again they racked their brains to remember everything Jesus said about what it is like to be his disciple. They remembered that when Jesus said, "Follow me," he also warned people of what that meant: "If any man would come after me, let him deny himself and take up his cross daily and follow me." [1] It was soon clear that it was not going to be any glory road. Each day would have its difficulties. Many of his disciples would end up being killed just as Jesus was killed.

Thus, long before the gospels were finally written, the followers of Jesus thought back to what he had said and done. They needed to know what they must do. Once they saw that death was conquered and Jesus was king of heaven and earth, everything he had done before took on new meaning for them. They could follow this king wherever his Spirit led. They had memories, stories, personal experiences, and the Scriptures to keep them on the path. They knew the ending. Now they had to figure out how to tell it from the beginning.

Begin with John the Baptist

Not everyone remembered the same things about Jesus in the same order. And some people told what they remembered in Aramaic, which was a kind of Hebrew, while others spoke Greek. What's more, each story had to be told in a way that would help a certain person or group of people catch on to what was really important. So the stories were told and retold for many years before they were written down. Even then people would tell something once more to make a point.

That is why our gospels are not exactly alike. Each evangelist told the story in his own way, just as preachers today do. They did not merely repeat what they heard or read. They were each

inspired by God to paint a scene with words so that the full picture of who Jesus really is could be seen clearly.

Nevertheless, all four gospels agree that Jesus' ministry did not really begin until after he had been baptized by John the Baptist. To be sure, Matthew and Luke tell us a few things about Jesus' birth and childhood, but somehow what John said and did was the right place to begin describing what Jesus said and did.

Not that all the gospels agree in every detail. Matthew suggests that according to Jesus, John was the new Elijah promised in the Scriptures,[2] but the Gospel of John reports that John the Baptist clearly denied that he was Elijah.[3] Just take a look at how each of the gospels describes Jesus' baptism. Even if you underline all the words that are exactly alike, you see that each gospel has its own special version of the story. But still all the gospels agree that if you want to understand who Jesus is and what it means to follow him, you must begin with John the Baptist.

Matt. 3:13-17
Then Jesus came from Galilee to the Jordan to John, to be baptized by him. John would have prevented him, saying, "I need to be baptized by you, and do you come to me?" But Jesus answered him, "Let it be so now; for thus it is fitting for us to fulfill all righteousness." Then he consented. And when Jesus was baptized, he went up immediately from the water, and behold, the heavens were opened and he saw the Spirit of God descending like a dove, and alighting on him; and lo, a voice from heaven, saying, "This is my beloved Son, with whom I am well pleased."

Mark 1:9-11
In those days Jesus came from Nazareth of Galilee and was baptized by John in the Jordan. And when he came up out of the water, immediately he saw the heavens opened and the Spirit descending upon him like a dove; and a voice came from heaven, "Thou art my beloved Son; with thee I am well pleased."

Luke 3:21-22
Now when all the people were baptized, and when Jesus also had been baptized and was praying, the heaven was opened, and the Holy Spirit descended upon him in bodily form, as a dove, and a voice came from heaven, "Thou art my beloved Son; with thee I am well pleased."

John 1:29-34

The next day he saw Jesus coming toward him, and said, "Behold, the Lamb of God, who takes away the sin of the world! This is he of whom I said, 'After me comes a man who ranks before me, for he was before me.' I myself did not know him; but for this I came baptizing with water, that he might be revealed to Israel." And John bore witness, "I saw the Spirit descend as a dove from heaven, and it remained on him. I myself did not know him; but he who sent me to baptize with water said to me, 'He on whom you see the Spirit descend and remain, this is he who baptizes with the Holy Spirit.' And I have seen and have borne witness that this is the Son of God."

Repent!

But what is so important about John the Baptist and Jesus' baptism? John seems to have been something of a prophet of doom, like one of those people wearing a sign saying, "The world will end tomorrow!" John preached "a baptism of repentance for the forgiveness of sins." He warned people to look out because they didn't have much time to get right with God. John said, "Even now the axe is laid to the root of the trees; every tree therefore that does not bear good fruit is cut down and thrown into the fire." People don't like to hear that kind of talk.

But the disciples remembered that Jesus thought John was absolutely right. They knew that Jesus did not need to be baptized in order to be forgiven,[4] but they remembered that Jesus had told them that John was the last and greatest of the prophets.[5] John came at the end of the old age. A new day, the dawn of the kingdom of God, came with Jesus, who said, "The law and the prophets were until John; since then the good news of the kingdom of God is preached." [6]

Even so, John was the right one to help bring in the new day by baptizing Jesus. That rough-and-ready prophet who warned people that the time was short had said, "Repent, change your ways, get ready for the kingdom, for God is about to take action." Later Jesus said, "Repent, change your ways, get ready for the kingdom, for God's action has begun." And when the early Christians started preaching, they said. "Repent, change your ways, and get ready for the kingdom, for the king has come!"

Like John, Jesus didn't waste his breath trying to please everyone. As Luke tells the story, when Jesus went to his home town, he read a part of the book of Isaiah to the people in the synagogue. They praised his nice words, but didn't really believe him and asked, "Is not this Joseph's son?" They were really saying, "Who does he think he is anyway?" When he warned them that God might well overlook them in favor of some other group that would accept him, as happened earlier in the days of Elijah and Elisha, they tried to kill him.

Jesus' disciples remembered that both John and Jesus talked straight and could be hard on people who only pretended to be religious. It was clear that Jesus' followers could be expected to speak out honestly, too, whether people liked it or not.

▍ Are you with me?

But Jesus' baptism by John means more than that they are like each other. All four gospels agree that the Holy Spirit came down upon Jesus. Jesus was a marked man. He had a special task. Like the kings in the Old Testament, he had been anointed by this act. He was the Messiah, the Christ. As the gospel writers looked back, they saw that from the beginning, Jesus was truly God's Son, the king of God's kingdom.

Jesus is such an unusual king that it is hard to remember that he is a king. He still doesn't look much like royalty to us either. Kings are supposed to be rich and have lots of servants. But Jesus did not behave that way, and he doesn't want his disciples to get fancy ideas either. His word is: "The kings of the Gentiles exercise lordship over them. . . . But not so with you; rather let the greatest among you become as the youngest, and the leader as one who serves." [7]

But even if he didn't look much like a king to most people, then or now, the gospels tell us that the evil powers in the world have known all along who he is. From the beginning, Jesus had to decide what kind of a king he was going to be. As the Son of God, he must have been tempted to use his power rather than to be obedient to God. And it wasn't long until Jesus crossed swords directly with the powers of evil. He showed he was a king with real clout: "They were all amazed and said to one another, 'What is this word? For with authority and power he commands the unclean spirits, and they come out.'"

What's more, Jesus got right down to the job of setting up his kingdom. That was what made people so angry and still does.

Jesus let them know that he was the anointed king who had come to preach good news to the poor, proclaim release to the prisoners, give sight to the blind, and bring liberty to oppressed people. In short, he had come to bring justice for everyone, just as the prophet Isaiah had said.

Whether you like it or not, King Jesus plans to make some big changes in the way things are going. He wants you to join with him, and when he closes the book and says, "Today this scripture has been fulfilled in your hearing," he wants to know. "Are you with me or not?"

If you are, then there are many exciting things to do. You will be working for the ruler of God's kingdom! But if you don't accept what Jesus has in mind or if you don't believe him when he claims to be your king, then, like the people in Nazareth that day, you may wish he would just go away. But he won't.

1. Luke 9:23
2. Mal. 4:5; Matt. 11:14
3. John 1:21
4. Matt. 3:14-15
5. Luke 7:24-35
6. Luke 16:16
7. Luke 22:25-26

Follow Me

Luke 5:1—6:16

Ready to follow

The world is full of smooth talkers trying to sell you something. You have to be careful. Learn to ask questions. Don't trust everyone who comes along. Otherwise you might be tricked and cheated by all kinds of false promises.

Unfortunately, the same thing is true in religion. God's people have learned the hard lesson that you can't trust every prophet who comes along. The words of a prophet must be tested. Is there some sign that this person can be trusted: Do the prophet's words and actions fit together? Do they fit with the long story of God and his people as told in the Bible?

Even Jesus' words and claims had to be tested. The Jewish people had to be careful. There had been phony prophets and messiahs from time to time. One of them had promised that the Jordan River would divide before him and his troops so they could walk into Jerusalem and drive the Romans out. But the Romans caught up with this "messiah," beheaded him, and took his head to Jerusalem.[1]

Another fellow got the Samaritans to believe that he was a new Moses who would lead them to the holy mountain. But Pontius Pilate, the same Roman official who sentenced Jesus to die, sent soldiers to deal with him and his followers. They killed those they caught, including the leaders who tried to flee.[2]

Jesus made strong claims, too. The early gospel writers re-

130

membered that people were cautious about believing him. In fact, some people rejected him without further questions. Even those with open minds thought twice before joining Jesus' campaign. What might Jesus do to show that he was really the king he claimed to be?

The miracle of the great catch of fish was just such a demonstration. Like the miracles in the Old Testament done by Moses or Elijah, the story is pretty hard to believe. But that is just the point. Everyone knew that only God, who created the world and the seas and all the creatures of the deep, could really control such things. Probably the farmers and fishermen understood this better than anyone else. Our friend Peter knew all about fishing. Yet he gave Jesus the benefit of the doubt and put out his net one more time.

The gospel writer wants us to know that the point of the story is not how many fish were netted. In fact, he doesn't bother to tell us what became of all those fish that were caught. No, the point of the story is that Peter caught on right away that Jesus had done something only God could do. Somehow God himself was present, just as he had been in the burning bush or when Moses' staff turned into a serpent or when he sent the plagues told about in Exodus.[3]

Like Moses, Peter was afraid. He saw that something new and mysterious had happened. He was convinced and so were James and John. They were ready to follow Jesus. Jesus' words and deeds fit with what God had been doing all along, but now God was taking direct action. This was not the time for doubt and caution. This was the time to get in on the act. So "they left everything and followed him."

The Son of man

Of course, a few boats full of fish could not convince everyone, especially people like the Pharisees and teachers of the law who were not concerned about fishing. Those people had read the Scriptures carefully, and they had some very strong ideas of what it would be like when God finally sent someone to save his people. Some of them had a particular biblical picture they liked best, a strange vision recorded in Dan. 7:13-14:

> I saw in the night visions,
> and behold, with the clouds of heaven
>   there came one like a son of man,
> and he came to the Ancient of Days
>   and was presented before him.
> And to him was given dominion
>   and glory and kingdom,
> that all peoples, nations, and
>   languages should serve him;
> his dominion is an everlasting dominion,
>   which shall not pass away,
> and his kingdom one
>   that shall not be destroyed.

This "Son of man" would also be the judge. He would forgive sins, and he would punish the wicked.

But most people expected this Son of man to come at the end of the world. They did not think God would bring his kingdom into the midst of this world. They were convinced that first he would destroy all wickedness, and then he would set up his kingdom with the Son of man ruling forever—they thought they had it all figured out.

As a result, the religious leaders in Jesus' day did not accept him because he didn't fit their ideas. They didn't understand what he was about, as when he helped the paralyzed man. They complained that Jesus should not tell the man that his sins were forgiven. Only God could do that. Jesus agreed with them. Only God could forgive sins.

That was just the point! Jesus was doing something only God could do. And he was doing it then and there on earth. What's more, he healed the paralytic to show that he knew what he was talking about: "But that you may know that the Son of man has authority on earth to forgive sins . . . I say to you, rise, take up your bed and go home."

Once again people were stunned by what happened. They were not as quickly convinced as Peter was by the fishing miracle. Still, "they glorified God and were filled with awe, saying, 'We have seen strange things today.'"

They certainly had seen strange and miraculous things. Jesus acted like the Son of man. But they expected him at the end of the world, and here he was announcing his kingdom now. Why didn't they all catch on as Peter, James, and John did, and join up with Jesus? Why didn't those religious leaders see that Jesus was the very one they had been expecting?

Luke goes on to show that some people did catch on, but the next person who left everything to follow Jesus was not exactly a religious leader. In fact, Luke tells us he was a tax collector. Tax collectors were regarded as traitors to Israel because they had sold out and gone to work for the hated Roman rulers.

Again, it did not seem to fit. Many of the religious leaders felt Jesus was showing concern and interest in the wrong kind of people. Evil people. No wonder they were angry with Jesus!

But Jesus answered, "Those who are well have no need of a physician, but those who are sick; I have not come to call the righteous, but sinners to repentance."

What would you have done?

People who don't play by the rules are not popular. Think about the way you run your life, the clothes you wear, the friends you have, or the things you believe deep inside. Most of us get pretty upset if other people come along criticizing us and telling us that things are going to be different from now on, especially if we think we're better than they are. We are likely to try to close our ears to the criticism. We may even say,

"We like to do things our way. Leave us alone." Finally, we may even get angry!

Jesus knows what people are like. We sometimes say, "Things are good the way they are. We don't want to change." Usually it takes real trouble before we're ready to try a new way. Most of us have to be quite sick before we finally go to the doctor.

We like to think we are in pretty good shape most of the time. People may be starving in Africa or dying of disease in India, but not many of us go hungry or get very desperate about surviving. It is easy for us to convince ourselves that we are in control, and we don't want anyone to change the rules.

So what Jesus said and did is a bit of a jolt to us too. He upset the religious leaders by having the wrong people for friends, healing on the Sabbath, and letting his disciples do a little threshing on the Sabbath. He was not doing things the way they were "supposed to be done." If he was right, then they were wrong. And what really made them angry was that he claimed that he could tell them what was right and wrong. He said, "The Son of man is lord of the sabbath."

There it was again! Jesus was doing what only God could do. He was controlling the fish in the depths of the sea. He was forgiving sins. He was changing the laws. The commandment said, "Remember the sabbath day, to keep it holy." And Jesus said, "The Son of man is lord of the sabbath." He was in charge! And the miracle was a sign of that.

By then people were not just standing around acting amazed. In fact, some of them were so angry that they were laying plans to destroy Jesus. But others had left everything to follow him because they were convinced that Jesus truly was the Son of man come to earth. Jesus chose his 12 apostles from among them.

It makes you wonder, doesn't it? All those people were naturally cautious and a bit doubtful at first, like most of us. And they had good reason to be careful. The Romans were rough on troublemakers. But after these claims and miracles of Jesus, people were either out to get him or ready to leave all and follow him. It makes you wonder. What would you have done?

1. Josephus, *Antiquities* 20:97-98
2. Josephus, *Antiquities* 18:55-57
3. Exodus 3–12

Now Hear This!

Luke 10:25-37; 6:17-49; 15:1-32

The master teacher

Jesus was a master teacher. The very fact that his followers were called disciples meant that they had come to learn from him. Like many religious teachers of that time, Jesus would frequently sit down with his disciples wherever they happened to be. Other people would crowd around to hear what the teacher or rabbi was saying to his disciples.

Sometimes students of the law of Moses would stand up and ask a question such as, "Teacher, what shall I do to inherit eternal life?" Then everyone would listen carefully to hear what Jesus said and how well he was able to interpret the Scriptures. Some people were so convinced by his teaching that they left their homes and jobs to follow him on to the next town.

Jesus was particularly famous for his parables or stories. They were short and simple, and even after his death and resurrection, his followers remembered them. Yet they also remembered that the parables were not always easy to understand. In fact, they were often more like riddles or surprise packages. You could carry them around with you for a long time before catching on to the secret.

The parable of the good Samaritan was told because a lawyer was trying to put Jesus on the spot. But by answering him with a question, Jesus got the lawyer to answer his own question about eternal life. The lawyer knew that the law of Moses said you should love God and your neighbor. But he wouldn't quit. He wanted a debate so he asked, "And who is my neighbor?"

Instead of spending the next two days arguing about that question, Jesus told a parable. The parable was full of surprises. In Jesus' little story the religious people, like the priest and the Levite who were supposed to know the law of Moses, never got around to helping the dying man. The Samaritan, who would have been an ignorant outcast from their point of view, took care of the man who needed help.

By the end of the story, Jesus had turned the question around, and again the lawyer had to answer him. Everyone could see that Jesus was saying, "Don't debate endlessly about 'Who is my neighbor?' That doesn't accomplish anything for God or man. What God is saying in his law is, 'Help those who need help. Be a neighbor.'"

The lesson was very simple, and the story helped keep the point clear. Ever since then, all disciples of Jesus have known that he was also speaking to them when he said, "Go and do likewise."

The kingdom is yours

Almost everyone agrees that Jesus was a great teacher, and yet he was not quite like any other teacher. In interpreting the Scriptures, he announced and described the kingdom that God had in mind for his people. If we think that Jesus' teachings are just a lot of lovely religious words, we have missed the point.

For example, many people love to read Jesus' "Sermon on the Mount," which is found in Matthew 5–7. This wonderful collection of his teachings is especially famous for the "Beatitudes" or blessings where Jesus tells us which people are truly happy and blessed by God. He mentions "the poor in spirit," "those who mourn," "the meek," "those who hunger and thirst for righteousness," "the merciful," "the pure in heart," "the peacemakers," and others.

But this sermon is more than sweet talk. Read through the rest of the sermon in Matthew and discover that Jesus combined his blessings with warnings to his followers about the difficult times coming and instructions about how they should behave.

The same sermon is reported in Luke, the gospel that we have been following. Again there are some differences in the way each writer tells the story. Luke suggests that Jesus gave the sermon on a level place or a plain instead of a mountain,[1] and he does not have so much packed into one speech.[2] But like Matthew, Luke wants us to see that in this sermon Jesus gave us straight talk on what it is like to be one of his disciples and to work for God's kingdom.

You have to admit that Jesus did not make any easy promises. Luke 6:17-49 is not an ad for a vacation resort. "Blessed are you poor . . . blessed are you that hunger now . . . blessed are you that weep now . . . blessed are you when men hate you, and when they exclude you and revile you, and cast out your name as evil, on account of the Son of man . . . but woe to you that are rich . . . woe to you that are full now . . . woe to you that laugh now . . . woe to you, when all men speak well of you."

Jesus was reminding his disciples of the same lesson that the people of God have learned and relearned through bitter experience over the years. When they have been rich, well-fed, jolly, and popular, they have become self-satisfied, believing they could run their own show without much help from God, if any.

137

That was true in the time of King Solomon and some of his successors, and it was true of many of the influential and powerful people in Jesus' time. They didn't want to accept Jesus as king or even allow God to change the way things were going. They were doing all right, and they figured that their success meant God was on their side. We still tend to think that way.

But look at the people Jesus called to follow him. Look at the people who turned to him for help. They were not the rich and successful but the poor, hungry, sorrowful, and outcast. They were the ones who were ready to admit that they were not in control of the world. Their best hope was that one day God would bless them. They had to believe that God was in charge.

Jesus was telling his disciples, "God has already blessed you. You are not high and mighty and famous, but you are in on the ground floor of the kingdom. You are lucky because you don't have wealth or social status to get in the way." What's more, Jesus was promising his followers that no matter what might come—sadness, persecution, sorrow, or even death—God would not abandon them. After his resurrection, Jesus' disciples remembered that promise with great joy!

But they also remembered that Jesus had some strong ideas

of how they were supposed to behave. They had been chosen to be his followers. That was a privilege. They had been blessed to be a blessing, just like God's people in other times. They were not to hoard all the blessings for themselves. They had been sent out to show kindness and love to others, even to people who were mean. They were not chosen to go around praying "Lord, Lord" while ignoring the needs of others.

No, Jesus was saying, God "is kind to the ungrateful and the selfish," and now they had been chosen to do the work of God's kingdom in the world. Again, this teacher made his point very clearly: "Be merciful, even as your Father is merciful."

Lost and found

Some of Jesus' teachings were nothing but pure joy for his disciples. The parables in Luke 15 certainly fit that description.

Luke introduces the parables with the comment that the religious leaders were complaining again about the company Jesus was keeping. When the early Christians were criticized, laughed at, and even attacked, they remembered that Jesus had also been persecuted and made to feel like an outsider. From the point of view of the religious leaders, Jesus and his disciples were not

part of God's people at all. But still they were confident of God's love for them. How could that be?

The parables of the lost sheep, the lost coin, and the lost son are a large part of the answer. Even if you have heard these stories a hundred times, they will have new meaning for you the day you feel really lost or left out or forgotten. Nobody gets scolded for being lost in these stories, not even the son who blew half of the family farm on wild parties. No, in all three parables Jesus insists that the most important thing is to find what is lost and to bring it back to safety,

So the shepherd leaves 99 of his sheep in the wilderness to go find the one that is lost. Why, that is incredible! What a foolish shepherd! He should hang on to the 99 good sheep and let the wolves eat the stray, right? And the woman turns her house upside down and calls her neighbors in for a party because she finds a lost coin. So what's the big deal? Why the fuss? Why the party? And the father sees his lost son coming and goes running down the road to welcome him home. It certainly is not what the son or we would expect. That shepherd, that woman, that father, all have one thing in mind: Save what is lost no matter what the cost.

Most of us would agree with the brother who stayed home. "Father isn't being fair. He has gone overboard." But if you are ever feeling lost, if all the "right people" get down on you, then remember the lesson Jesus taught. God, our heavenly Father, is not only fair, he is much more than fair. He is loving. He is concerned. And when we are lost, he has only one thing in mind: to save us.

Some people, like the elder son or the religious leaders who criticized Jesus, want God to be fair, but nothing beyond that. In fact, they don't want God to take extreme measures for anyone. But the story is as old as Abraham and Moses. God intends to save the oppressed, the outcast, the sinful, even if he has to take extreme measures to do it. And like the man who finds his sheep, the woman who finds her coin, and the father who finds his son, all of heaven is filled with joy when one of us is found: "Just so, I tell you, there is joy before the angels of God over one sinner who repents."

1. Matt. 5:1
2. Luke 11:1-4, 9-13, 33-36; 12:22-34

Who Do You Say that I Am?

Luke 7:1-35; 9:7-36

The secret

People have always argued about things that are important to them, especially politics, money, and religion. All of us have strong opinions about things that influence our lives. So it is no surprise that people have not always agreed about who Jesus really was or is. Sometimes people have disagreed so violently that they have gone to war, persecuted, tortured, or even killed each other to win the argument.

Even now, some people think Jesus was a fraud. Others say he was a great teacher or even a prophet. But Christians insist that he was more than just a prophet or a teacher. He was God's Chosen One or Messiah and he is still Lord of our lives.

Of course, we can say these things with confidence because we have already heard the story of Jesus. We know how it came out, and by the grace of God we have learned to trust that story.

In fact, we peeked at the last chapters of Luke's gospel and found out how the story ends before we went back to put the pieces together. What's more, most of us have gone to church on Christmas and have heard how the angels spilled the good news to Mary and the shepherds: "He will be great, and will be called the Son of the Most High," [1] and "for to you is born this day in the city of David a Savior, who is Christ the Lord." [2]

But during Jesus' ministry the disciples were often confused about him. Even after his resurrection, most people did not know the whole story from beginning to end. They had probably only heard bits and pieces, perhaps about his baptism by John, or his parables, or a miracle. Most likely they would have heard about his death, and perhaps they would have heard that his disciples believed he was still alive. How could they put the pieces together? How could they make them fit with the long story of God and his people that they knew from the Old Testament?

No wonder people were so confused about Jesus. They could not see the big picture. Jesus' role in the long story was a secret to them. All they had were hunches, about which they argued long and hard. Many people are still arguing about hunches.

Who are you, Jesus?

Hundreds of years before Jesus was born, there was a prophet in Israel named Elijah. In the Old Testament, 1 and 2 Kings are filled with marvelous stories about Elijah and his successor, Elisha. In Chapter 10 of this book we learned how Elijah was swept away by God in a whirlwind and how the prophet Malachi said that Elijah would return before the end of the world.[3] Remember the stories you read about Elijah feeding the widow and her only son with a jar of flour and a jug of oil that just didn't run out? Remember how Elijah prayed to God and stretched himself out on the dead child and the child came back to life and Elijah delivered him to his mother?[4]

The Jews remembered. And you can be sure John the Baptist remembered because some people thought he was Elijah. So imagine the excitement when Jesus came upon a funeral procession for the only son of a widow, and he raised him to life and gave him to his mother! You can almost hear the crowd gasp. Many were whispering, "Elijah!" But they didn't say it out loud. Luke tells us, "Fear seized them all; and they glorified God, saying, 'A great prophet has arisen among us!' and 'God has visited his people!' And this report concerning him spread through the whole of Judea and all the surrounding country."

John's question

When the word got to John, he was in prison. Herod was about to have him beheaded. Poor John! It looked as if he

142

wouldn't live to see God's judgment on the evil world that he believed was so near. Perhaps he was even wondering if he had been wrong about God and Jesus. Many of God's prophets had been troubled by such doubts before.

John's time was running out. He couldn't wait to see what Jesus would do next and then make up his own mind. So he sent two of his disciples to Jesus with the question, "Are you he who is to come, or shall we look for another?"

Jesus' answer may seem strange at first, but it hit the nail on the head: "Go and tell John what you have seen and heard: the blind receive their sight, the lame walk, lepers are cleansed, and the deaf hear, the dead are raised up, the poor have good news preached to them. And blessed is he who takes no offense at me."

Jesus did not say that he was Elijah. But he told John that all these things which were promised in the prophecy of Isaiah were happening.[5] At the very beginning of his ministry, Jesus had announced to the people in Nazareth that he was there to fulfill those prophecies.[6]

No, Jesus was not trying to evade John's question, nor had he turned his back on his friend in prison. In fact, he went on to make a public speech praising this man who was about to be executed. As Luke tells it, Jesus knew that such a speech would not be popular with some people and was probably quite dangerous. He said that some people will never like the music no matter what you play. No matter what you do, those same people will pick you apart: "For John the Baptist has come eating no bread and drinking no wine; and you say, 'He has a demon.' The Son of man has come eating and drinking; and you say, 'Behold a glutton and a drunkard, a friend of tax collectors and sinners!' Yet wisdom is justified by all her children." Remember that! God's wisdom will prove to be trustworthy no matter what public opinion may say.

But the question did not die with John. In fact, now it was John's murderer, the wicked King Herod, who had heard what Jesus was doing and was worried that John had come back to haunt him or that he would have to contend with another Elijah or some great prophet. By this time, Luke tells us that Jesus had also stilled a storm, driven out a demon, healed a woman from excessive bleeding, and raised a little girl back to life.[7] And the next thing we hear, Jesus had fed a crowd of 5000 with five loaves and two fish—with plenty left over!

Raising children back to life, feeding people with supplies that don't run out—no wonder people thought that Jesus was Elijah. But notice the difference. The people who followed Jesus were beginning to hope and believe that he really was the one God had promised. But Herod and his crowd were not really interested in Jesus or his mission at all, except that he might be a threat which needed to be eliminated.

The chosen one

So who is this Jesus? It is all very fine to hear what Herod thought or some newspaperman has guessed. But like John the Baptist, we do not have forever. Let's hear from someone who knows, someone who was close to Jesus, someone who was there.

Luke does not keep us in suspense any longer. In Chapter 9 of his gospel, he reaches back into the memory bank of the early Christians and brings out a block of material that had already been stored in Mark's gospel.[8] Luke retells two stories and some words of Jesus which put the pieces together.

The first story is about Peter. When the disciples were asked what people were saying about who Jesus was, they reported what they had heard: "John the Baptist; but others say, Elijah; and others, that one of the old prophets has risen." But when Jesus directed his question at them, Peter was the spokesman: "And he said to them, 'But who do you say that I am?' And Peter answered, 'The Christ of God.'"

There is the answer. Jesus is God's anointed one, his Messiah, his king. Peter spoke for those who had been closest to Jesus and had seen what he was doing and heard what he said. So that settles it, right? Not quite.

Jesus did not allow his disciples to rush out and tell the world that he was the Christ of God. Instead, he tried to make them understand that he was not going to be the kind of king that they or the crowds probably had in mind. They had to keep the secret until Jesus had finished his mission. And he was going to do it God's way, not the way of glory that people were expecting: "The Son of man must suffer many things, and be rejected by the elders and chief priests and scribes, and be killed, and on the third day be raised."

Jesus was the king, all right. Peter was correct. He was the Christ whom God had sent to set up his kingdom. But he was going to be a king who would suffer, and his subjects were warned that they must be ready for hardship and even death, too. But the day of glory, the day when King Jesus would reign, would not be far off: "But I tell you truly, there are some standing here who will not taste death before they see the kingdom of God."

The second story tells of a wonderful vision that Peter, John, and James had, and it is one of the most amazing stories in the Bible. Up on a mountain, "heavy with sleep" but keeping awake, Peter and the others saw Jesus' face and clothing shine with light. They also saw Moses and Elijah appear with him discussing Jesus' "departure, which he was to accomplish at Jerusalem."

What they were talking about was Jesus' death and resurrection. Then the voice of God came out of the cloud saying, "This is my Son, my Chosen; listen to him!" Here was Moses, the one who gave the law, and Elijah, the most important of the prophets, helping Jesus prepare for his death. But it was not going to be an ordinary death. The Greek word that Luke used for "death" or "departure" can also be translated as "exodus." Moses and Elijah knew what an exodus was. It was God's way to save his people. What's more, many years before, they had heard God speak to them out of the cloud, too.[9]

Now we know. Like Moses and Elijah, Jesus was chosen for a special mission. Like the kings of the Old Testament, he was anointed. But there is more to it. We can't just put up a marker on that spot and stay there as Peter first wanted to do. No, the mystery is deeper than that. Jesus is far greater than Moses and Elijah. He was chosen for his work long before he was even born. He was God's Son and he was king in a way no king had ever been or ever would be. What Jesus said was God's own word, and God's Spirit was with Jesus from beginning to end as he went about bringing God's kingdom.

So don't tell anyone yet! People will just misunderstand. Wait until the whole mission is accomplished, until Jesus' suffering and death are over, until God has raised him up to rule the whole universe. Then it will be clear who Jesus really is. "And they kept silence and told no one in those days anything of what they had seen."

1. Luke 1:32
2. Luke 2:11
3. Mal. 4:5-6
4. 1 Kings 17
5. Isa. 29:18-19; 35:5-6; 61:1

6. Luke 4:16-21
7. Luke 8:22-56
8. Mark 8:27—9:13
9. Exod. 33:7-11; 34:29-35; 1 Kings 19

Chosen to Serve

Luke 9:51—10:24; 10:38—11:23; 18:1—19:27

Kingdom messengers

Jesus did not try to do everything by himself. In later years his followers remembered that he had given them important work to do even while he was still busy with his own ministry. As they looked back on those days, the disciples could see that he had been preparing them to carry on the work of his kingdom.

In Luke 9:51—19:27, we find Luke's account of Jesus' long journey from Galilee to Jerusalem. Actually the distance is not so far, and if you read straight through these chapters, it seems as though Jesus is taking forever on the trip. But here is where we find out what we are supposed to do once Jesus is gone. Luke lets us hear what Jesus told his disciples to do: announce the kingdom, pray and worship together, take care of those who need help, and be prepared for the return of the king!

But announcing the kingdom was not all that easy. In the old days, the herald or announcer would come into a village ahead of a king and shout, "Get ready, the king is coming." Then everyone was to come out and welcome him. If they didn't, the king might burn the town to punish their disobedience.

Jesus' disciples were his announcers. "He sent messengers ahead of him, who went and entered a village of the Samaritans, to make ready for him." But the people didn't want to have anything to do with this king who had made up his mind to go to

Jerusalem. They were Samaritans, and Jerusalem was the capital city of their rivals, the Jews. Also, they knew that any king who planned to march into Jerusalem was as good as dead already.

In any case, the first time the disciples tried to be heralds, it didn't work. And they were probably embarrassed and angry. They wanted to punish the Samaritans for not receiving their message. "Lord, do you want us to bid fire come down from heaven and consume them?" But Jesus did not act like other kings.

The king's orders

No, announcing God's kingdom was to be a bit different. Carefully read Luke 10:1-16 again, and notice the orders this king gave. He sent his unarmed messengers ahead, equipped only with his word of peace. When people received them, they healed the sick and assured the town that "the kingdom of God has come near to you." But when they were rejected, the messengers did not strike back or do any violence. They left, taking nothing with them, not even the dust they picked up in the streets.

Yet they did leave a warning: "You have had your chance. We did our job. We brought the kingdom to you, and you rejected it. So be warned. God destroyed Sodom and Gomorrah when they refused to listen. And God will be especially hard on those of you who should have recognized God's kingdom when it came!" This was a terrible warning with its words of fire and brimstone and Hades. No one likes to hear that kind of talk.

But Jesus was playing for keeps! His messengers were not asked to judge others or to punish anyone. In fact, Jesus rebuked his disciples when they tried to take that power in their own hands. Announcing the kingdom meant waging war with the evil forces of greed, hatred, and sin which opposed God's kingdom and his king. That was why, when the disciples found they could defeat the evil powers, Jesus said to them, "I saw Satan fall like lightning from heaven."

Still, the joy of this kingdom is not the defeat of others. Jesus warned his disciples not to take their delight in overpowering evil spirits. We are not sent out to make ourselves look powerful or important or smart. The point is that we are in the service of the king of heaven and earth. Our names "are written in heaven." And even though we who follow Jesus are not all as wise as prophets or as powerful as kings, we have been chosen to be messengers of God's kingdom.

Pray!

Jesus was a man of prayer who taught his disciples how to pray. That does not mean that they walked around with their hands folded all the time. But Luke's gospel tells us a great deal about Jesus at prayer and what he taught his disciples about prayer.

The parable of the Pharisee and the tax collector in Luke 18 made it very clear that Jesus did not want people to pray just to hear themselves talk. The straight talk of the sinner who admitted he was a sinner was better than the smooth words of a hypocrite who trusted himself and prayed to himself.

Jesus taught his disciples the "kingdom prayer" or "Lord's Prayer" which told them what it is really all about. And ever since, his followers have glorified God, prayed for God's kingdom, and asked for daily bread, forgiveness, and freedom from temptation until the day the kingdom fully comes. In churches, hospitals, prisons, homes, submarines, and spaceships, God's people have thanked God for all he has already done, prayed for his kingdom to come, and asked God to help them in the meantime.

Jesus also taught that prayer is crucial because it is the way God's people keep in touch with headquarters. Sometimes Christ's followers get so involved in the important work of the kingdom and in trying to get others to do things their way, they forget to listen and share and learn. Once Jesus had to remind one of his disciples, Martha, that her sister Mary really had the right idea when she took time to listen to him. So prayer was important to Jesus as a way of knowing that what he was doing would help bring in God's kingdom. He emphasized that we need to pray for the same reasons.

But God's people have an advantage which Jesus mentioned several times in talking about prayer. That is, God's people know that he cares and will listen to what they say. Jesus did not promise that God would always give us exactly what we request, but he assured his followers that God has good things in store for his people. In effect he said, "Don't hesitate to ask. Bang on heaven's door if you must. Pester God if you have to. He will listen."

Well done, good servant!

One day, God will establish his kingdom, once and for all. We do not know exactly how or when. But because we are sure of God's final victory, it has always been very tempting for Christians to try to figure out God's timetable.

People have had all kinds of theories. Some have taken their Bibles and made charts to try to "crack the code." Some have decided they have the answer, and have even taken groups of people up to the tops of mountains to welcome Jesus on the day he was "supposed to come." But just as it is not our business to try to punish those who reject the kingdom, so it is not our business to determine when the kingdom will finally come. That is God's business.

Even in Jesus' time some people thought they had it all figured out, and they could not understand why Jesus kept "wasting his time" with all those people on his way to Jerusalem. So, "he proceeded to tell a parable, because he was near to Jerusalem, and because they supposed that the kingdom of God was to appear immediately."

This parable is a harsh story of a nobleman who "went into a far country to receive a kingdom and then return." The story centers on the king's servants and what they did while he was gone. Some were very successful, and some did a decent job. But one of them was so concerned about what the king would do when he returned that he never got down to his work. And the king was very angry with him.

As Luke tells the story, it is a warning to servants of King Jesus to stick to their business. Instead of rushing out to punish people who reject the kingdom, or guessing and wondering about when Jesus is coming, his disciples are told to care for people who need help, to continue praying and watching for the kingdom, and to announce that the king has come and is coming again.

Jesus set the pattern himself. He told people about the kingdom. He prayed and suggested that people keep looking for

clues that God's kingdom was already present with them.[1] And even though he knew that his time on earth was short, he took time to care for the sick, the lonely, and the outcasts who needed him along the way.

We may all have our theories about when the kingdom will come or the world will end or Jesus will return. And we may have some strong ideas of what things will be like then. But Jesus does not want us to waste our time trying to figure all those things out. He has not even prepared us very well for such guesswork. But he has given us work to do, and he is serious about this responsibility. He has invited us to share in the work of his kingdom. We have been chosen to announce the kingdom, to pray and watch for the kingdom, and to offer help to all who need it in the meantime.

And when that day comes, that great and glorious day of the Lord, the best words that any of us could hear would be, "Well done, good servant, well done!"

---

1. Luke 17:20-21

Hail to the Chief

Luke 19:28—20:40

The king enters Jerusalem

When a head of state visits another country, he is met at the airport by an honor guard, the roll of drums, and a military band playing his country's national anthem. After words of welcome, the long line of sleek black limousines with motorcycle escorts ushers the illustrious visitor to his destination. Throngs of people crowd the sidewalks, cheering and shouting and waving flags or handkerchiefs as his car sweeps by.

Presidents, kings, and rulers have always been welcomed with great fanfare. In ancient empires like Rome, they did it with real style. First came armies, caged wild lions and tigers, slaves, and gladiators. Then came the emperor himself seated high on a throne carried by slaves, and all the people shouted, "Hail Caesar! Hail Caesar!"

When Jesus arrived in Jerusalem, the capital city, he also made an impressive entry. He arranged for a special colt that no one else had ever ridden. His disciples decked it out with their robes, and he rode into the city in the midst of the fanfare of people who welcomed him as king. They waved palm branches, made a carpet for the colt with their robes, and shouted, "Blessed is the King who comes in the name of the Lord! Peace in heaven and glory in the highest!"

Jesus' entry into Jerusalem might not have looked impressive to a Roman who had seen Caesar in a triumphal procession, but

many Jews recognized that Jesus came as the prophets had promised the king would come. When Matthew tells the story of Jesus' entrance into Jerusalem, he mentions the Old Testament prophecy from Zech. 9:9-10.

> Rejoice greatly, O daughter of Zion!
> Shout aloud, O daughter of Jerusalem!
> Lo, your king comes to you;
> triumphant and victorious is he,
> humble and riding on an ass,
> on a colt the foal of an ass.
> I will cut off the chariot from Ephraim
> and the war horse from Jerusalem;
> and the battle bow shall be cut off,
> and he shall command peace to the nations;
> his dominion shall be from sea to sea,
> and from the River to the ends of the earth.

The people loved what they saw. Luke tells us that these were the people who had seen Jesus' mighty works. They were convinced. This was the king, the Prince of Peace, the Son of God! Hail King Jesus!

But not everyone was filled with joy. Luke indicates that some of the Pharisees in the crowd did not approve of this display and said to Jesus, "Teacher, rebuke your disciples." To which Jesus replied, "I tell you, if these were silent, the very stones would cry out." Jesus refused to spoil the joy of the occasion.

Of course we might have expected the Pharisees to disapprove. Throughout the gospel we have seen growing opposition against Jesus. Religious leaders like the scribes, Pharisees, and teachers led the opposition. But why? Why were such people unwilling to accept him? Those who should have welcomed the Messiah ended up plotting to kill him.

Tears for Jerusalem

The story of God and his Chosen People has many sad chapters. The fact that Jews and Christians have often rejected God's love is not new. Sometimes Christians have tried to make themselves feel better by claiming that the Jews killed Jesus. Like any kind of race hatred, this hatred of the Jews (anti-Semitism) is evil and has produced much suffering.

Jesus, his disciples, and most of the people in the crowds that loved him, were all Jewish. These people accepted him as the

155

Messiah or king that God had promised to send to his people. They were the ones who cheered and threw their robes in the street when he entered Jerusalem. Some of them saw the risen Jesus and went out as announcers of his kingdom. And they were all Jews.

But like the prophets before him, Jesus also experienced rejection and closed minds on the part of God's people. Certainly there were many good things about the Pharisees and other religious leaders. No doubt most of them were sincere about their religion and tried hard to keep God's law. They read their Bibles, said their prayers, and looked for God's kingdom.

But some of them relied on the rules more than they trusted God. Some did not expect God to do anything very new. They thought they had it all figured out, and Jesus didn't fit their idea of God's Messiah.

For this reason, as he approached Jerusalem, Jesus wept for the city. He could see that self-righteous, self-satisfied people would not accept God's kingdom of peace. They would rather do it their own way, and Jesus knew that way was leading to destruction.

He sensed that people would try to kill him because they thought he was a troublemaker, a threat to peace. They were afraid to be associated with anyone who talked about a "kingdom," especially where the Romans might hear. They could not believe that God would take such extreme measures to bring peace to his people.

Yet Jesus only pressed the point further. As Luke tells it, the next thing that Jesus did was to enter the temple and drive out the money changers. This king went right to the center, to the house of God. Note that Jesus did not go to King Herod's palace or to the Roman courthouse. Instead, he laid claim to God's throne and drove the salesmen out of the courts of the Lord.

But even that kind of a kingdom was unacceptable to many of the religious leaders. They had a good thing going. They did not want Jesus or anyone else telling them how to run the temple. The Roman rulers were letting them manage the temple affairs, so who was Jesus to come along and try to clean things up?

The next thing they knew, Jesus was teaching in the temple.

He wasn't going to go away. He was going to continue to give them problems. One way or another, he would have to be eliminated: "The chief priests and the scribes and the principal men of the people sought to destroy him; but they did not find anything they could do, for all the people hung upon his words."

The Jerusalem trap

The end was in sight. We already know how this part of the story ends, so why wait around for the trap to snap? What difference does it make how Jesus' enemies got him? They got him. What more is there to say?

This last lesson on Jesus' ministry brings us face to face with the ugly side of people. The story is not pretty. People like you and me can be terribly cruel. We can scheme to hurt other people, and sometimes it happens that other people lay a trap for us, even if we have not deserved it. We cannot ignore the cruelty of the real world.

The story of God and his Chosen People faces the sad and terrifying facts of life. God's Son knew what it was to be hated and victimized by evil people. The one who now is king of heaven and earth was once trapped, betrayed, and put to death.

In Luke 20, Jesus' enemies circled like wild beasts waiting for the kill. But Jesus did not just give up. In fact, by the end of the chapter, it is clear that Jesus had won the round. His enemies would have to find some other way to get him.

They came at him with questions that appeared to be worth asking: "Who is it that gave you this authority?" "Is it lawful to pay taxes to Caesar or not?"; "What will happen to marriages in the resurrection?" But they were not asking honest questions. They just wanted to pin something on Jesus, but he exposed their dishonesty.

In the first case, he answered with a question about John the Baptist. It was a good place to begin a serious discussion about Jesus' authority since John had baptized him at the beginning of Jesus' ministry. But they were sullen and suspicious and refused to answer. They had already made up their minds and did not want to discuss hard questions.

Then Jesus warned them with the frightening parable of the owner of the vineyard and the rebellious servants. He let them know they were making a mistake in rejecting him. But that only made them more furious. Like all prejudiced people, they had closed their minds.

Jesus escaped their trap again when they asked about paying taxes. Maybe Jesus was smiling a bit to himself when he said, "Give Caesar what belongs to Caesar and give God what belongs to God." Now they would have to decide what was Caesar's and what was God's.

He also knew that the question about the resurrection was a trick question. The Sadducees did not believe in the resurrection. He showed them that they had not read their Bibles carefully, and did not let them catch him with a phony problem.

Time after time Jesus kept them at bay. Amazingly, he even gave worthwhile answers to their dishonest questions. And his followers learned important things from those unusual answers. Jesus was no fool. He knew that his enemies refused to be convinced. It was only a matter of time before they found a way to get rid of him.

So once again we are back where we started with the story of Jesus. The sin and evil of the world produced his death. He died because God's people were caught in the web of sin, and they continued to weave the evil net by selfish and cruel efforts to trap and kill him. You and I are part of that same network in our cruelty and selfishness and prejudice.

It appears that sin and death can never be defeated. Certainly you and I can't do it. That's the awful truth. But remember, on that cross God has already done it. That's the gospel truth.

It's a New Day

Acts 1:1—2:24, 37-42

▮ Chosen to be apostles

Many years passed between the end of Jesus' ministry and the time when the gospels were written. In those years, important and exciting things continued to happen. The book of Acts tells us about those years.

It appears that the same person who wrote the gospel of Luke also wrote Acts. This early Christian writer, usually identified as Luke, tells us that God continued to help his people spread the news of the kingdom by means of his Holy Spirit. For in spite of what the world had done to his Son, God did not abandon us. No, God's Spirit, who had been with Jesus in his work, now came to be with Jesus' followers. There was still work to be done, and God continued to choose people to serve him in this world.

The Acts of the Apostles is exciting reading, especially if you have followed the story of God and his Chosen People from the beginning. In these lessons, we will only read a few chapters, but if you keep reading you will find amazing things: miracles, shipwrecks, jailbreaks arranged by angels, magicians, people who lie and cheat and are punished with death, and the repeated announcement of the reign of the good and loving king who rules heaven and earth.

As you read, you will notice once again that this book, too, is really about people. Good people, bad people, the sick, the powerful, the believers, and the people who hate God's king-

159

Peter preaches on Pentecost

dom are all in the story. The apostles whom Jesus chose to send out to tell the world the good news play leading roles in the book, especially Peter and Paul who are featured as leaders of the apostles. As the author of Acts tells it, Peter stood out in the first years of the mission; Paul became more important when the Christians were working in countries that were a long way from Jerusalem.

Good old Peter. Let's begin with him. Luke remembered him as the sturdy fisherman who first caught on to who Jesus was the day of the miracle of the big catch of fish.[1] He was the one who first declared that Jesus was "the Christ of God." [2] And he saw Jesus on the mountain with Moses and Elijah and struggled to know what to say.[3]

Peter was a man of faith. He believed in Jesus—trusted him. In fact, he promised to be true to Jesus even if he had to face prison and death. But Peter was also the one who folded when the going got rough. Under pressure, he denied that he even knew Jesus.[4]

Peter was a saint, but not perfect. He was much like you and me. But God's story is about people like us. Somehow God's Spirit can work through imperfect people. God, who chooses people like us, must love his people very much.

Called to be witnesses

There are Christians today who can't seem to think of anything except when the world will end and what that will be like. At times, Jesus' disciples also got all wrapped up in the idea that Jesus had come to bring the end of the world, or at least to throw out the Romans and set up a palace in Jerusalem. According to Acts, the last question that Jesus' disciples asked before he was taken up to reign in glory was, "Lord, will you at this time restore the kingdom to Israel?"

But Jesus' answer pointed in a different direction. He told them that wasn't their business. Instead, he laid out their marching orders. Probably each of us should memorize Acts 1:7-8: "He said to them, 'It is not for you to know times or seasons which the Father has fixed by his own authority. But you shall receive power when the Holy Spirit has come upon you; and you shall be my witnesses in Jerusalem and in all Judea and Samaria and to the end of the earth.'"

161

Those words turn out to be a good outline of the book of Acts. Once the Holy Spirit had come, the apostles began preaching, worshiping, and caring for the needy in Jerusalem. They were Jesus' witnesses right in the city where he was killed. They did acts of kindness and peace and love. As Acts tells it, they remained in Jerusalem until they were driven out by persecution.[5] Then with the enabling and urging of the Holy Spirit, they expanded their work to Judea and Samaria and beyond.[6] Eventually they got as far as Rome.[7]

But all of that was still to come. Once Jesus was gone, the disciples could not stand around on the mountain waiting for him to come back. No, Jesus had promised that they were about to be commissioned for a tremendous task. They needed to make preparations to carry on the work of the kingdom. So they organized along with the rest of Jesus' followers. They gathered to pray, to study the Scriptures, and to select someone to take Judas' place. They were ready. Now it was up to God. They did not try to get started under their own power.

The birthday

The second chapter of Acts presents the marvelous story of Pentecost, the birthday of the church. This was one of the most joyful days in the history of God's people, complete with miraculous tongues of fire, amazing communication across language barriers, powerful preaching, and thousands of people whose lives were changed. As the author of Acts tells it, the witnesses of Jesus were off to a great start.

But in the midst of it all, some people made smart remarks and said, "They are filled with new wine." Certainly the disciples were not drunk, but in a way of speaking, they were filled with "new wine." Remember in Luke how Jesus warned that "new wine" would burst old wineskins?[8] What was happening to the disciples was so new and inspiring that none of the old ways of being religious fit. Even the serious-minded people who could see that something amazing was happening asked, "What does this mean?"

Not everything that happened on Pentecost can be easily explained. It is not even clear in the book of Acts. For example, did those people who "spoke in other tongues" actually speak in languages that they had never learned? Certainly the author of Acts wants to tell us that the Holy Spirit worked a special miracle, and whether it was a miracle of speaking or hearing, people who were visiting in Jerusalem from all over got the message—the whole world would hear how God raised Jesus and made him king.

Pentecost was the day when the Holy Spirit came upon the followers of Jesus, to remain with them and us. Remember how the Spirit came upon Jesus in the form of a dove at the beginning of his ministry? [9] And remember how John the Baptist said, "I baptize you with water; but he who is mightier than I is coming, the thong of whose sandals I am not worthy to untie; he will baptize you with the Holy Spirit and with fire."? [10]

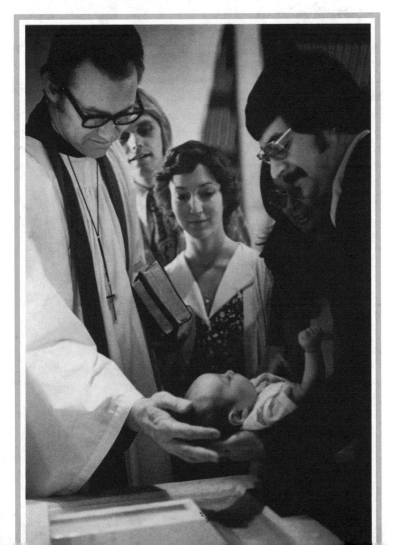

Now the "mightier one" had come and gone, and he had sent the Spirit. And this time the Spirit was in the form of fire.

Of course, not all Christians have such amazing religious experiences. Over the years, some people have "spoken in tongues," and some have had other experiences of the presence of the Holy Spirit.

But on Pentecost the Holy Spirit came for all Christians as Jesus promised. It was the birthday of the church. Everyone who was baptized in the name of Jesus Christ on that day received "the gift of the Holy Spirit," whether they spoke in tongues or not. Indeed, something new happened for all of us in Pentecost. For when we were baptized, we also were given the Holy Spirit.

If you read Chapter 2 of Acts, you see that the author only gives 14 verses to all the display, but he gives twice as many verses to Peter's sermon. Read it carefully. Notice how much Peter uses the Scriptures. And notice how the story of Jesus is at the center of what he has to say.

Peter said Pentecost was the beginning of the time spoken of by the prophet Joel—the beginning of the end. It was a sign that God was at work. God's Spirit was inspiring men and women to tell people to change their ways, and God was promising to forgive and rescue his people once more.

If this sounds like a sermon you have heard before, don't be surprised. Part of the good news about God is that he is so amazingly patient with us. His offer of love and salvation just doesn't quit as long as there is hope for us. God has hope for us long after we have given up.

And another part of the good news is that God enables us to say "Yes!" to him. The story of Pentecost is the story of God's Spirit helping people who had a part in Jesus' death to find forgiveness. Perhaps that was the real miracle of Pentecost. A new day had dawned. God had raised Jesus from death and made him king. He had sent his Spirit. And God is still at work in the world. He never gives up.

---

1. Luke 5:1-11
2. Luke 9:20
3. Luke 9:28-36
4. Luke 22:31-34, 54-62
5. Acts 1:12—8:1
6. Acts 8:1—9:31
7. Acts 9:32—28:31
8. Luke 5:37
9. Luke 3:22
10. Luke 3:16

Dangerous Business

Acts 5:12—8:3

▪ Martyrs

Sometimes you have to stick your neck out. It could result in your being roughed up or even killed. But when it comes to what is right and wrong, there are times when you must speak out even if everyone else gets angry at you for not keeping your mouth shut.

People do not always like to hear the truth. God's followers have learned that lesson time and time again. When the prophets criticized false religion, some of them were imprisoned and killed. When Martin Luther spoke out against false teaching, he had to go into hiding so that some of the leaders of the church would not burn him at the stake. No doubt you can name others who have been persecuted or even killed for speaking the truth.

The first followers of Jesus quickly found out that many people were not ready to listen to their message. They were witnesses to the good news of God's kingdom which Jesus had gotten under way, but it was not easy to be a witness. The Greek word for "witness" was "martyr," and so many "witnesses" were persecuted or killed that the word came to mean "someone who dies for what he or she believes." Jesus' followers soon learned that when he said, "You shall be my witnesses," [1] he was giving them a difficult task. And we have been chosen for the same task.

But God's people have also learned that he does not give them

165

difficult and dangerous tasks to do and then forget about them. No, even in the suffering and pain—especially in the suffering and pain—God is present with his people.

Sometimes God's presence has been amazing and spectacular, as when Peter's shadow seemed to have power to heal, or the time an angel helped the apostles escape from jail. Only God knows why he does not always step in with such miracles to rescue his people from pain or death. Yet, again and again, God's people have been able to see signs that he has not abandoned them.

Arrested again

In the Acts story, Peter and the others had just been freed from prison by the angel when they were arrested and hauled into court again. The judges were furious. They had told the disciples to keep quiet, and had thrown them into jail to make sure they would be quiet. Those judges were also the religious leaders, and they did not appreciate having a ragtag group of fishermen and tax collectors spreading the story that religious leaders had conspired to kill Jesus. They were not about to let such talk continue, even if it was the truth.

Then Peter and the others answered, "We must obey God rather than men!" And he preached a little sermon on how God raised Jesus "to give repentance to Israel and forgiveness of sins." Face to face with people who were ready to kill him, he found the courage to tell those religious leaders that God would not let him remain silent, and he had the grace to tell them of God's forgiveness.

Where had fainthearted Peter found courage to speak like that? Peter saw it was the presence of God's Spirit that gave him such courage, and he said so: "And we are witnesses to these things, and so is the Holy Spirit whom God has given to those who obey him." Jesus had promised that they would be given wisdom and the right words for just such tough times.[2] The followers of Jesus could see that God was with them.

The judges were ready to kill the apostles on the spot. But God sent help. Just when it looked as if the mob would kill them, a person who was not even a Christian was given the courage to speak. He was a Pharisee. Even though he was not convinced that Jesus was the Messiah, he was inspired to say,

"Wait! Be careful! What if God really is at work? If these people are fakes like some others we have seen, their cause will fail. But if God is with them, we shall never be able to stop them anyway. Wait: time will tell. But we dare not risk opposing God!"

And what is most amazing is that the religious leaders did wait. The disciples were beaten up as a warning and were told to keep still. No angels rescued them from that beating. But the witnesses could see that God was with them. So they continued to speak out boldly, obeying God but disobeying the judges.

Problems

Since the first days of the church, Christians have learned that they do not always agree. Some people think that Christians should always be pleasant and agreeable. Perhaps that would be nice, and certainly many quarrels among Christians have been vicious and destructive to the work of God's kingdom. But Christians have also discovered that even their disputes can be used by God.

According to Acts 6, there was a quarrel between two groups in the church. The "Hebrews" were probably Jewish Christians who had always lived in and around Jerusalem. The "Hellenists" were probably Jewish Christians who came from cities and countries where Greek was spoken. At any rate, these two groups could not agree on how food and other necessities should be distributed. It was the kind of problem that could have split the church into two angry groups. Such a fight would have made a very poor impression on other people in Jerusalem.

The apostles saw the problem and tried to settle it quickly because they did not want to be distracted from their preaching. They didn't try to hang on to all the power, either. They asked the rest of the disciples to choose seven leaders to work out the problem. They laid their hands on them and prayed for the people who were chosen. But, as Acts tells it, that was not the end of the problem.

One of those who were chosen to solve the food problem, Stephen, turned out to be a gifted preacher as well. The Holy Spirit had helped the church find and recognize this leader from among the Greek-speaking Christians, the "Hellenists," and the church had solved the quarrel about the food. But the Holy

Spirit was already at work on a much bigger matter. Stephen would stir up such a hornet's nest in Jerusalem that the church would be forced to take its mission to other places.

Stephen

It was one thing to have local people like Peter and the apostles preaching about Jesus and criticizing the religious leaders. That was bad enough. But when a "Hellenist" like Stephen started to talk that way, people became angry all over again. They were suspicious of those who spoke Greek or dressed like the Greeks. Such people were not welcome to make statements about their religious leaders or to tell them what to believe. And so Stephen, with his wisdom and Spirit-filled speeches, made the citizens of Jerusalem very angry. They wanted to kill him.

The story of Stephen's death shows us the ugly face of prejudice. It may seem surprising, but it was probably other Greek-speaking Jews like Stephen who got everyone stirred up against him. They knew what to say. They knew that people thought that the Greek-speaking Jews did not respect Moses, God, the temple, and the Law. People were afraid that the Hellenists would try to change their religious customs. So Stephen was accused of all of those things.

When Stephen got his chance to answer the charges, he took the opportunity to be a witness, and he was "martyred" for that witness. Acts tells us that Stephen made a very long speech in answer to the charges. His speech is really a sermon on the history of God and his people, beginning with Abraham right up to the time of Jesus. Acts 7:1-53 is a good review of our story to this point.

Stephen reminded his audience that God's Chosen People have been unfaithful again and again throughout history and frequently persecuted or killed the very people whom God sent to help them. Then he drove home the point: "You have betrayed and murdered, too. In fact you killed the very One whom the prophets announced beforehand. You have the law, all right, but you did not keep it."

It was the truth, but they did not want to hear it. So they dragged Stephen out of town and stoned him. Acts tells us that as he died, Stephen had a glorious vision of Jesus at the throne

of heaven, and he prayed for God to forgive his murderers. But such a death was not a pretty sight.

The death of Stephen was the beginning of a great persecution against the other Christians in Jerusalem. And a certain young man named Saul was organizing efforts to get rid of the Christians.

Still, as they looked back on it later, the disciples could see that even in the midst of the terror, God had not deserted his people. Stephen's life had not been spared, but he died aware of God's presence with him. And even the persecution could be seen to fit into God's plans.

Fleeing for their lives, the witnesses scattered throughout the region of Judea and Samaria. Apparently the Holy Spirit was using the pain of this experience to give birth to the next part of the mission of the church. Remember the words of the Lord, "You shall be my witnesses in Jerusalem and in all Judea and Samaria and to the end of the earth"? Even in the face of persecution and death, the mission of the kingdom was advancing.

1. Acts 1:8
2. Luke 21:14-15

Friend or Foe?

Acts 9:1-31; 15:1-29

A changed man

Do you believe that a person can really be changed? Have you known anyone whose life was different after something important happened? According to some people you should be suspicious about anyone who claims to be a changed person. "You can't teach an old dog new tricks," they say. For the most part, such caution is good advice. If somebody cheats you or says bad things about you to others, you are going to be a little slow about trusting that person the next time.

Put yourself in the place of Ananias. He had heard about this man Saul who had been glad to see Stephen killed. Ananias could see that Saul was a wild-eyed, self-appointed defender of the law of Moses, and he knew that this enemy of God's kingdom was out to hunt down Christians. Clearly Saul was dangerous! He was to be avoided like sin itself.

But then Ananias had a vision in which the Lord told him to go find Saul in a particular house and heal him. Saul? There must be some mistake. Vision or no vision, it just didn't seem to make sense, and Ananias said so. But the Lord said to Ananias, "Go, for he is a chosen instrument of mine to carry my name before the Gentiles and kings and the sons of Israel; for I will show him how much he must suffer for the sake of my name."

Saul as God's "chosen instrument"? Saul chosen to be a witness to the Gentiles? Incredible! No wonder Ananias had his doubts. Saul was such a super-Pharisee and defender of the law of Moses. Why would God choose him of all people to preach the gospel to the non-Jews? Poor old Ananias must have been shaking his head in confusion and fear as he went out to find Saul.

The story of the call of Saul, which is the Jewish name for Paul, is one of the most amazing stories in the whole Bible. It must have amazed the early Christians, too, since the story was retold two more times in the book of Acts.[1] Of course Paul himself also mentioned it several times in his letters.[2] When you read those accounts, you will be able to see that the story was told several ways to emphasize different things. But the point of the story was always clear: God chose an enemy of the gospel to become one of its most effective servants.

And it did not take long before Paul's old friends saw the change. They had cheered him when he went out tracking down Christians. They knew what a capable person he was and how well he understood the Scriptures. But now he showed up in their synagogues trying to convince people that Jesus really was the Messiah. And when he got back to Jerusalem, he continued to preach about Jesus. He even took on the people who had stirred up the mob against Stephen. Paul really had been changed. His old friends didn't approve of the change and they tried to kill him. The Christians had to be cautious, but they ended up protecting Paul by first smuggling him out of Damascus in a basket and later taking him out of Jerusalem for his own safety. Was he worth all the trouble?

Nobody knew just how God was going to use this newly chosen servant. Paul had been called in a strange way. But before long the Christians could see that he was an excellent choice. He loved God's law and had studied the Scriptures carefully. Certainly, God must have had a special task in mind for this new convert.

The apostle to the Gentiles

The first Christians were all Jewish. They went to the temple in Jerusalem for special events whenever they could. They worshiped every Sabbath in the synagogue. They celebrated the Passover with their families, and circumcised their baby boys when they were eight days old. Jesus had done the same things, and the Christians believed that he was the Messiah God had sent to save Israel.

Many of those Jewish Christians believed that God also wanted to save the rest of humanity. They were willing to tell Gentiles, that is non-Jews, about Jesus. After all, many Gentiles had become Jews before. They circumcised the men and boys in the family, learned the Jewish prayers and worship, and ate only the foods which the Scriptures said they could eat.

The first Christians just assumed that all believers would be Jewish like them, or at least all Gentile Christians would first become Jewish. But the Holy Spirit began to stir things up again in the church. Just when life was getting comfortable in Judea, Galilee, and Samaria, the Holy Spirit was getting ready to prod the church to bring the gospel to the ends of the earth.

As the book of Acts tells the story, Peter was first troubled by a very strange dream. He was told to eat some foods that Jews were never supposed to eat. Then the Spirit told him to go and preach the gospel to a Gentile. You can find this interesting story in Acts 10:1-48. The point of the story is that now all nations were being included in the Chosen People.

But it was Paul who made it an issue for the whole church. He was the kind of person who wanted things to be clear. So when some people said that all male Christians had to be circumcised and that all of the law of Moses had to be kept, Paul and his helper Barnabas asked for a church convention.

Though many people find it difficult to get excited about church conventions, important changes often happen at such meetings. In recent years, many Christian churches have worked hard to make their witness effective, and most Christian groups have begun to appreciate and be thankful for the witness of other churches. Church conventions helped make these changes, and such changes make a difference. The Holy Spirit is still at work.

That first church convention also had to face a tough decision. The meeting is generally called the Jerusalem Council, and scholars think it took place around A.D. 49. Unfortunately, the New Testament doesn't bother to tell us exactly when the meeting happened, but at least the book of Acts gives us some details in Chapter 15.

Now the door was opened. Paul was given a clear signal that he could preach to the Gentiles and they would not be required to keep all the Old Testament laws. The Gentiles were asked not to eat strangled things because that was particularly offensive to Jews. And they were asked not to eat food sacrificed to idols because other Gentiles might think they were worshiping that idol. But basically, Paul was free to tell his new converts that they did not need to give up their national identity to become Christians.

Paul had forced the issue. And as Acts informs us, the Jewish Christian apostles could see that the Holy Spirit was leading them to a new day. "It has seemed good to the Holy Spirit and to us," they said. That first church convention was not as dramatic as Pentecost or the stoning of Stephen, but the Holy Spirit was just as surely at work. The excitement of what had happened must not be lost. Now Paul was ready to carry the gospel to the end of the world. He had been called by God, chosen to serve. The church would never be the same again. The Holy Spirit had seen to that.

Of course, not all changes are good. Sometimes people and things change for the worse. Certainly there are good reasons for being careful about cheering every time something is new or different. And God's people have wisely learned to hang on to traditions and hymns and good friends that have proved to be trustworthy.

But the story of Paul's calling as the apostle to the Gentiles clearly shows that people can be changed by God. Things do not always have to remain as they are. Even when you may be ready to write someone off as an enemy or give up on what looks like a lost cause, don't forget Paul. God called an enemy of the gospel to be its champion and friend. Or when you are ready to decide that your own life will never amount to much, remember—God does not accept such verdicts. He continues to work his miracle of change in people and churches, even when they and others may have given up. He can even use enemies and conventions to help bring his kingdom into the world.

The early Christians learned that lesson from Paul and others. After the Jerusalem Council, the other apostles were ready to encourage their former enemy on his mission to people that were not Jewish like them. They believed that Paul really had been changed by God, and now the church would change, too.

1. Acts 22:4-16; 26:9-18
2. Gal. 1:13-17

Hang On to the Gospel

Galatians 1:1—2:21

Reading Paul's mail

Did you ever find a trunk full of old letters in your grandmother's attic? Did you sit down and read them and try to figure out what life was like for those people? Maybe some were love letters or announcements of marriage or new babies or deaths. Or maybe the letters told of a serious disagreement or problem that happened long ago in your family. Whatever they were about, reading old letters is interesting because it gives you a peek into someone else's life. Of course you have to be careful about whose mail you read!

The New Testament is full of old letters. Some are more like little sermons than letters, but several are very personal notes from one Christian to another or from an apostle to a congregation. Even if you don't usually read other people's mail, go ahead and read these letters. The early church saved them for you to read.

As many as 14 of those letters have been associated with Paul. Probably Paul did not write all of them himself. His secretary and his followers may have written some of them in his name, and one of them, the letter to the Hebrews, doesn't even have Paul's name on it. But people were not so interested in who wrote what in those days. What they were concerned about was to hang on to the gospel that Paul preached.

Paul's early letters are the oldest books in the New Testament. A personal note to Philemon about a runaway slave and his letters to the churches in Thessalonica, Galatia, Corinth, Philippi, and Rome were probably written around A.D. 50-60. Remember, that's 10 to 20 years before the gospels were written.

Letters had to be carried by a messenger and were written on expensive handmade paper or leather in those days. So people only sent letters when they had a good reason to do so. Paul's letters show that he usually wrote to help congregations deal with a problem. Some scholars have spent their lives studying Paul's letters and the problems to which they were addressed.

For now we shall focus on just one letter, Galatians. From it we can quickly get an idea of what is so interesting about Paul and his letters. Don't let that stop you from peeking at other letters in the New Testament mail bag. Each letter is a slice of life from the story of God and his people.

The free gift

Paul was angry. When he wrote to the churches in Galatia, he made it plain that he did not like what he was hearing about them. After a few short lines of greeting, he accused the people of deserting the gospel. Paul was telling them straight out, "Shape up."

Why was he so angry? Apparently some Christians were not willing to accept the decision of the Jerusalem Council. They had come into the congregations in Galatia after Paul had gone. Now they were telling these Gentile Christians that Paul was not preaching the true gospel. They did not trust Paul or his message and accused him of being a phony apostle. They said he was just operating on someone else's orders. Who was he to say that Gentiles don't have to be circumcised or obey the Jewish food laws? These opponents claimed that God would only save the people who kept all of the laws in the Old Testament and that Christ was the Messiah only for the Jews.

Think about it. If those people were right, none of us would qualify as Christians. Even today there are people who may ring your doorbell and claim that your church and pastor have it all wrong. They will say that you must worship on Saturday and quit eating pork, for example, or you will not be saved.

Paul let them have it with both barrels. It is no wonder this letter is sometimes called the declaration of Christian freedom.

The whole point of the letter is that God's love and forgiveness is now for everybody. When God raised Jesus, he started a new era.

As you read what Paul was telling the Galatians, think what it means for you. Paul is saying again and again that you don't have to do anything to "qualify" for God's love. Through what Jesus Christ did, God gave his favor, his love, to everyone. He began with the Jews. They had been his Chosen People since Abraham. But you don't have to become Jewish or anything else to be eligible. Through Christ, God offers his love to you.

The power of his love

In the first two chapters of Galatians, Paul opened his case against his opponents. It was a bareknuckled fight, and Paul

began by defending himself. From the first line on, he was out to prove that he was truly an apostle "not from men nor through man, but through Jesus Christ and God the Father, who raised him from the dead." He used strong words. Even today some Christians think Paul was a bit too bold. But he was not trying to "win friends and influence people." He was seeking to serve Christ.

Paul had to defend himself against the charge that he was just taking orders from some church executive in Jerusalem. So he gave a blow by blow account of his life, beginning with his persecution of the Christians. He emphasized again and again that he did not even get instruction in the faith from the big shots, and that he was not impressed by people's reputations anyway.

In his own words, Paul described his call to be an apostle, and it must have been a tremendous experience. After it had happened, he could see that God had set him apart for this call before he was born, just as the Old Testament prophet Jeremiah had been set apart before birth.[1] Neither he nor the other apostles had planned on that event. They could only stand back and glorify God for bringing about such a change.

Paul always had an intense love of the law of Moses. But now he saw the law in a different way. He could deal with anyone who tried to lay down laws or conditions or qualifications that people need to meet to earn God's love. He could say, "I've been down that road, and I was good at it too. But all of that is in the past." Now Paul could see that doing the right thing at the right time or keeping the law did not make him worthwhile before God. His driving ambition to keep all the rules did not justify him, did not qualify him for God's kingdom.

Now he could see that God had already accepted him, and judged him worthy. This was not because of his loyalty to the law but because of what God himself did through Christ Jesus. God had made a new covenant, a new arrangement. But it took a special revelation of God to help Paul see the light.

What's more, Paul could see that you can't have it both ways. If you are going to try to earn God's favor by playing it by the rule book, you are going to be suspicious about the idea that God already decided to extend his love to all people. You are going to doubt that God's Messiah, Jesus, has really saved us from having to prove ourselves good enough for God. And you are going to want to keep all the rules, just to "play it safe!"

That is just what Paul accused Peter (Cephas) of doing. Paul told the Galatians that once Peter got a bit wishy-washy about the law when some very strict Jews came to town from Jerusalems. The result was that the rest of the Jewish Christians, including Paul's friend Barnabas, set themselves apart from the Gentile Christians in Antioch in order to obey the law. Then all the Gentiles probably thought they were supposed to keep the whole law too.

But Paul said, "No!" When God raised Jesus from the dead, he showed the world the power of his forgiving love. Instead of striking back for Jesus' death, God did just the opposite.

Just as he had planned all along, God was saying, "I accept this innocent death as the perfect sacrifice. My Messiah, Jesus, has now fulfilled all the requirements of my law."

Paul had not been willing to believe that message until confronted by God with a revelation. But once Paul got the picture, he was more than ready to spread the good news to the whole world, not just to the Jews.

And Paul was not going to let anyone get the message confused. There was no reason to go back to the time when people tried to earn God's love by keeping the law. That had never been the purpose of the law anyway. Anybody who tried to make Christians play that game was just plain wrong, and Paul would tell them so. And Paul meant *anybody*, including big shots from Jerusalem or Peter or people who were troubling the churches or even an angel from heaven.

The gospel is clear. God has already told us of his love through his Messiah, Jesus. And now God has sent us his apostle to make sure we don't get the message confused. Hang on to the gospel!

---

1. Jer. 1:5

Who Can You Trust?

Galatians 3:1—4:31

Paul the theologian

By this time you have read several different parts of the Bible. You have seen how the story of God and his people has been woven into histories, poems, prayers, and prophecies by those who wrote the Scriptures. But you have probably already noticed that Paul's letters are a bit different from those other books.

Paul was a theologian. He had been trained as a Pharisee to interpret the Scriptures and had a keen mind for discovering what the Scriptures meant. Of course, he knew the stories of the Old Testament and no doubt he had heard a great many of the stories about Jesus. But it is one thing to tell the stories, and it is another thing to explain how all the pieces fit together. Paul was good at that.

In Chapters 3 and 4 of Galatians, Paul was trying to stretch the minds of the Christians in Galatia. He saw that they needed to really examine their faith so that they wouldn't be babies who believed everything that anyone told them. And Paul has been helping Christians grow up ever since.

The promise comes first

The first thing that Paul did was to give a lesson in Old Testament history. He probably wanted to let the Galatians see that he understood the Old Testament better than his opponents

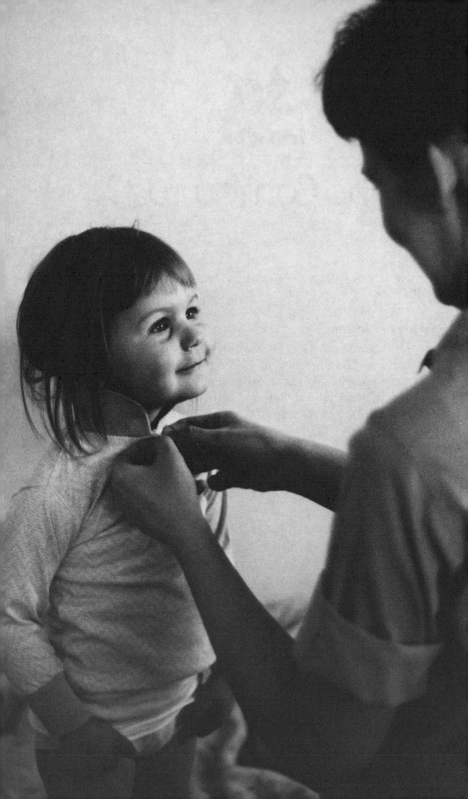

who were so fired up about getting everyone to keep the law. But Paul also showed that the best way to understand Jesus was to study the Old Testament. You can almost hear Paul making his case to his audience:

"When God chose his people, he started with Abraham. Right?"

"Right."

"And God started right off by making a glorious promise to Abraham, 'In you shall all the nations be blessed.' Correct?"

"Correct!"

"And Abraham had never heard of the law of Moses. That came 430 years later. Abraham didn't try to qualify for God's favor. God chose him, and Abraham trusted God. All Abraham had was his faith in God."

"So?"

"So right from the beginning God only asked Abraham and all of his children to trust him. Trust or faith was the basis of God's relationship with his Chosen People from the very first. God was planning to bless all the people on earth on the same basis. Only faith."

Paul wanted to drive home the point that God was good to Abraham and his children simply because he is gracious and he chose to love them. And what God began with Abraham, he completed through Abraham's greatest descendant, Jesus. Now the promise had been fulfilled. Now through Abraham and his offspring all the nations in the world would be blessed. And the whole thing was built on faith—God being faithful to his promise and people trusting God.

But a long time passed between Abraham and Jesus. God's people needed guidance and help until the promise was fulfilled. And that was what the law of Moses was for. The law was never intended to be the last word from God. It was a good word, and it still is. Many parts of the law of Moses are still the best guide we have to what is right and wrong. God knows we can use the help.

But the problem is that many people would rather play it by the book than trust God. You know how that goes. What if you don't like having someone in authority over you, or you resent a person's power over you? Aren't you tempted to say,

"Listen, tell me the rules, and I'll follow them. Just don't bother me!"? That way, you can be in charge, more or less. And you can also let the boss know if you think somebody else—maybe even the boss—isn't playing by the rules. Then you've beaten him at his own game.

But suppose the person in charge came along and said, "Look, I've decided to change the system. All along I've been more concerned about the people than the rules anyway. I've made arrangements so that from now on all you have to do is trust me. The rule book won't make my decisions about you."

Would you like that? Would you believe it? What if the "arrangements" were very convincing? What if you had begun to discover that the boss was really concerned about you? Do you think you could depend on the boss the way you used to rely on the rules? Could anyone be that trustworthy?

Paul wanted the whole world, including you, to know that God keeps his promises. The name of the game is faith, trust in God. He made his promise to Abraham, and he lived up to his promise to bless his Chosen People by giving them the law to regulate their lives. But that was only one step in the long story.

God had a much grander idea. Both his promise to Abraham and the law he gave to Moses pointed forward to the day when he would send his son, Jesus, as the Messiah. Jesus was God's way of making all of us his Chosen People, his children. Everyone could look at Jesus' life, death, and resurrection and see that God is trustworthy. In a sad and troubled world where people break their promises, betray, and even kill each other, God keeps his word.

And those who trust in Christ have inherited God's promise to Abraham. We are all chosen, just as the sons of Abraham had been God's Chosen People. And since the promise is for everyone, the old restrictions have been dropped. As Paul put it: "There is neither Jew nor Greek, there is neither slave nor free, there is neither male nor female; for you are all one in Christ Jesus. And if you are Christ's, then you are Abraham's offspring, heirs according to promise." We are all one in Christ Jesus. God delivers on his promises. That is good news for all of us.

Free in Christ Jesus

There are some advantages to being a baby. Your parents do everything for you. They pick out your clothes, clean up after you, feed you, wash you, and take care of you. You are free just to lie around watching the bright lights and waiting for the next meal or nap. You never have to make any tough decisions. What a soft life!

Of course the other side of the coin is that when you are a baby nobody asks what you think. Your family can decide to move to France and never consult you. Or if somebody decides to dress you up in a clown suit so everyone can take pictures and have a good laugh, there's nothing you can do about it, except bawl, which only makes the pictures funnier. What an insult! You want to protest, "Kids are people too!"

Even as you are growing up, other people still do a lot of thinking for you. Remember when you were afraid of the dark or thought there was a tiger hiding in your closet, or used to cry when there was thunder? Someone older had to convince you not to be afraid of such things. It's all part of growing up.

In Chapter 4 of Galatians, Paul wrote about growing up. He could see that the Christians in Galatia were attracted by the security of living under the law. Paul tried every way he knew to show that this was a great mistake. The whole chapter is really four different arguments.

In Gal. 4:1-7, Paul reminded them of what it is like to be under a guardian. You are the heir, all right. Your father promised the money to you in his will. But until the day arrives that your father set for you to get control, you must take orders from the guardian. In the same way, the law was the guardian for God's children until the day God sent his Son. Now the day has come, and the wealth of God's promise goes directly to you —even you Gentiles who were adopted into God's family. The guardians are out of a job. Don't let them make all your decisions anymore.

Then in verses 8-11, Paul told them to remember how superstitious and afraid they used to be. They were probably the kind of people who did whatever their horoscopes told them. Or maybe they read tea leaves or were afraid of black cats. Whatever those "weak and beggarly elemental spirits" were,

Paul could see the Galatians were getting superstitious again about calendars and holy days. They wanted a code or rule book. They were afraid to trust God. They wanted some additional security, just in case.

So Paul gave a personal plea. He felt badly that these opponents had upset the Galatians. He begged them to remember the hard times and good times they had gone through together. Paul was worried.

Finally he told a little story about Hagar and Sarah to try to make his point. He called it an allegory, which meant that all the parts of the story were supposed to symbolize something else. Clearly Paul was stretching the account in Genesis and he knew it.

But after you have figured out how the allegory works, don't miss the point that Paul was making. God wants his children to be free, not slaves of anybody or anything. We have been chosen to serve, all right, but not like machines or pawns that just follow orders. Neither are we supposed to be running scared as if the stars or evil spirits are out to get us. No, God has called us to live in a relationship with him, like princes and princesses in the home of a king. He wants to bless us, not curse or enslave us. And he has promised to let us share in the kingdom work of bringing his blessings to the whole creation. If you can't trust God, who can you trust?

Free! Free! Free!

Galatians 5:1—6:18

▓ Free to trust

Paul was the great apostle of Christian freedom. As you read his letters, you will find that again and again he fought to defend the gospel of Christian liberty. Somebody always wanted to "improve" the gospel by listing all the things that you have to do to be a Christian. One group thought you had to have special mystical knowledge. Another group thought all real Christians should speak in tongues. And Paul's opponents in Galatia tried to make all the Gentiles become like the Jews.

You might think that Paul would have become tired of the struggle. No doubt he did. It was hard enough to keep moving from town to town all over Asia Minor. He was frequently beaten up by Romans and Jews who did not believe Jesus was the Messiah. He was thrown in prison several times, shipwrecked three times, and often cold, hungry, and in danger. Still, the Holy Spirit kept him going.[1]

The message that God gave to Paul must still be announced loud and clear. God wants us to be free people. He sent his Son to break the bonds of sin, fear, and death which enslave all people. And once Christ has given us our freedom, why would we listen to anyone who wants to put our spirits in some kind of straightjacket again?

That was what made Paul so angry with his opponents in Galatia. He warned that if they got circumcised "just to be safe,"

they would be showing that they didn't have faith in Christ. He said, "If you receive circumcision, Christ will be of no advantage to you." Strong talk! And so is his comment, "I wish those who unsettle you would mutilate themselves!" Somehow we don't expect to find that kind of statement in the Bible.

Paul was not concerned about circumcision in itself. The fact that today, for health reasons, boy babies are circumcised before they leave the hospital would not have bothered him. In fact, he said, "In Christ Jesus neither circumcision nor uncircumcision is of any avail."

But the problem comes when people get circumcised or do something else because they don't really trust the gospel. They would rather play it by the book or live by the law, and they say to themselves, "What if we both believe in Jesus and at the same time go through all the motions? Then God couldn't possibly reject us."

When people try to tell God what he can or cannot do, they have refused to believe what he has already done. The message is clear. If you are going to play it safe and rely on the rules, you better keep all the rules! No exceptions, or you lose. But if you believe God and trust in his Messiah, then what's all the fuss about?

God is not our enemy. We do not have to jump through hoops or stand on our heads to make peace with him. God has already made peace with us. That's what the gospel of Jesus Christ is all about. If you can't trust God, who can you trust?

Free to love

Paul was a strong defender of Christian freedom, but he also saw that a Christian is not free to do just anything he wants. Some people like what Paul said about Christian freedom but don't want to listen to what he said about Christian responsibility. They say, "But I thought you said we are free. Now you start talking about the law of Christ and about shutting off 'the desires of the flesh.' Why can't we just do whatever we please?"

What about it? Does it seem as though Paul was talking out of both sides of his mouth? On the one hand he said that God saved us through Christ and that we did not save ourselves by keeping the law. If we try to save ourselves by keeping the law, we are being foolish and refusing to trust God.

On the other hand, he said that God's Spirit still encourages us to hang on to the central message of the law, "You shall love your neighbor as yourself." That means that things like immorality, enmity, envy, and drunkenness are to be avoided by Christians. And love, joy, peace, patience, and kindness are good things for us. But all that is pretty obvious. Even people who aren't Christians would agree that the things on the first list are bad and the things on the second list are good. So what happened to Paul's strong talk about freedom?

Think about it in this way. Suppose two teenagers are both invited to join a gang which is planning to rob a store. It sounds like easy money. Still, they both know that robbery is wrong, so they both say no. But their reasons for saying no are different. One of them knows that if her parents ever found out, they would throw her out of the house forever. She knows she has to play it straight to be on their good side. The other teenager says no because he knows that his parents trust him and count on him to do the right thing. He knows that they love him, and he thinks too highly of himself and them to do such a thing.

Paul saw that our reasons for doing things are important. If we obey the Ten Commandments because we are afraid that God will "get us" if we don't, we shall always be slaves. And we shall probably resent the list of "dos" and "don'ts." We will be acting out of fear in order to keep God from punishing us. That is a poor way to live if there is a choice.

God has given us a clear choice. Remember how in the Old Testament the promise came first and then the law? Well, the same thing continues in the New Testament. God loved us first, so we can love others. Because God showed that he is trustworthy and that he cares for us, we can see that even the law is based on love. We try to "walk by the Spirit" and do what is right because we already "live by the Spirit" with the good news of God's love supporting us every day.

Free to care

People who are perfect don't belong in the church. If we think we are perfect, we tend to believe we don't need help from anyone. We are often critical of others. If we won't admit that we have made some mistakes, we won't accept forgiveness

193

from anyone. What's more, we will expect everyone else to be perfect like us!

But the church is not a society of perfect people. In fact, the story of God and his people shows again and again that all of us need forgiveness from God and from each other. And the good news is that God has already reached out to accept us. In fact, he took extreme measures by sending his Son to tell us of his love and bring his forgiveness. We are not in a position to look down our noses at others. But we are in a position to let others find out about forgiveness because we have been forgiven.

Paul and the other early Christians knew very well that they were not perfect. They soon saw that they still made mistakes even after they were Christians. Paul knew that some of the Christians in Galatia were making the terrible mistake of turning away from the gospel. Maybe Paul himself was wrong in being so rough on his opponents.

But Chapter 6 of his letter to the Galatians shows that Paul did not expect perfection. He did not try to get all the people who were wrong thrown out of the church. Instead, he reminded the Galatians to care for each other and to be gentle with those who had made mistakes, and he closed his letter with words of blessing. The key word for the church was and is *love*. In one of his most famous chapters, 1 Corinthians 13, Paul went so far as to say that love is the greatest spiritual gift that Christians have.

Even now, almost 2000 years after Paul wrote to the church in Galatia, God's people still are not perfect. Each new generation has had to admit this. Cheating, lying, cruelty, and war continue, even war in God's name. But is that a reason for giving up?

No, the story of God and his people is a story of God's love for sinful humanity in a broken world. We are loved by God. He sent his Son into this world to assure us of his concern and bring his forgiveness. And we have been given each other so we, too, can love and be loved again. Part of love may be telling someone when he is wrong, as Paul did. Part of love may even mean suffering or dying for someone else, as Jesus did.

But God's servant Paul has taught us to cling to the freedom

of the gospel. And our love and concern for each other is the quiet signal that God's kingdom is present among us. Even in this world which is often confusing and uncertain, God's love remains with us.

Will God ever set up his kingdom for all the world to see? Will there ever be an end to sin and death and evil? Will God's people always have to struggle with only the quiet presence of his love to support them? How long, O Lord, how long?

1. 2 Cor. 11:21-32

The End?

Revelation 1:1-20; 21:1—22:21

▮ The vision of John

Every story must have an ending. In one sense, the story of God and his people has already ended. God sent his Messiah, raised him from death, and set him on the throne above heaven and earth. That part of the story is done. But Christians also know that the kingdom of God and his Christ will never end.

Time moves on, and the world is still full of crime, war, greed, and immorality. We are still part of the story, and we want to know where it will all end. Why doesn't God just put a stop to the evil? When will God's Messiah show the world who really is in charge?

The last book in the Bible is called "The Revelation to John" or "The Apocalypse." It is the story of a prophet's vision and probably was written sometime around A.D. 90-95. The author was a faithful Christian named John who had been banished by the Romans to a little rocky island called Patmos. John no doubt knew that the Romans had destroyed Jerusalem and killed most of the people in the city about 20 years earlier. He may even have heard about the heroic efforts of some Jews to hold out against the Roman legions, fighting until the last person in the temple died. They had been sure that God would rescue them at the last moment, but John and the rest of the world knew that they had been slaughtered.

And now the Romans were trying to get rid of the Christians.

Anyone who wouldn't say a little prayer to the emperor was suspect. The Romans thought such people were not loyal to the state or were maybe even planning a revolt. They had to be hunted down and eliminated.

The Christians were in trouble. They were willing to pay taxes and pray to God for the emperor. But the emperor was not God. Caesar was not the Lord of heaven and earth. "Jesus is Lord," they said. But the Romans did not like that kind of talk. So for the next 250 years, the Romans tried to bring the Christians in line with pressure, exile, torture, and many public executions. It certainly did not look as though Jesus were Lord.

But the Christians were prepared for such hard times. They had seen that Jesus himself had not been spared suffering. They remembered that he had warned that there would be persecution. They had been given the book of the Revelation to John. Once again God had provided for his people.

John's vision was a strange mixture of beasts, angels, fiery horses, dragons, and lambs, but still it was a word of comfort and hope. It was good news for people who were struggling with powerful forces that threatened to destroy them. The message was clear: *No matter how terrifying life might become, God is still in charge, and one day he will set up his kingdom for all the world to see!*

The reign of terror

Do you ever think about the end of the world? Do you believe that pollution will choke out life on this earth or that humanity will destroy itself with thermonuclear warfare? What will the future be like? Will the people of the world learn to live in peace with each other? Will there be enough food and fuel?

Well, the Revelation to John has good advice for God's people. It starts right off talking about "what must soon take place" and promises blessings to all who read and hear the prophecy. Of course, the book is primarily about what was going to take place "soon" around A.D. 90. That was long ago.

But still today, especially in hard times, people who read or hear the prophecies often find that it gives them hope. People who have been in prison for their faith or are in fear of death have turned to this book for comfort because it was written for people in trouble.

In particular, John's vision concerned seven churches in Asia Minor that were facing hard times.[1] The message was this: Be faithful to the Lord; terrible things are going to happen, but the Lord will win the final victory.

John wanted God's people to know that the ancient prophecies were still true. Remember what the Old Testament prophets Ezekiel and Daniel had dreamed? The Son of man would come on the clouds dressed in shining clothes and displaying all his glory.[2] But now the Christians would know that this "Son of man" was the Lord Jesus. In the end God and his Messiah would be in charge. God was and is the beginning and the end, the Alpha and the Omega.

But that did not mean that life would always be easy. In fact, John could see that the forces of evil were about to begin a reign of terror. Christians would be attacked. Even saying "Jesus is Lord" might mean death. The future looked very bad. The book is not bedtime stories for children. It is frightening. It is a stern call to believers to continue to trust God even at the cost of life.

Most of the Revelation to John was a vision of how bad the future would be. The Christians were told to prepare for the worst: famine, inflation, wars, plagues, torture, and death. One of the famous word pictures used was that of the four horsemen who ride out to plunder and destroy the earth.[3] Another image was of the scroll which was unrolled slowly so that each of seven seals was broken one at a time.[4] John also spoke of the seven angels and seven trumpets which signal the coming end.[5] And there was even a war in heaven between Michael and the angels and the dragon with seven heads, ten horns, and seven crowns.[6]

Many of those images were code pictures for Roman emperors and others who were trying to eliminate the Christians. People who gave in and prayed to the emperor as Lord were people who "worshiped the beast and its image." They had turned their backs on Jesus, the Lamb of God, and they refused to trust Jesus as Lord.[7] John saw that such people who tried to save their own skins were in danger of being totally lost.

In the long story of God and his people, this book is a strong reminder that the story is not over yet. In fact, people still are tortured and killed for what they believe. Often Christians have been guilty of fighting on the side of the forces of evil. God's people have not always been faithful, and frequently they have forgotten that they have been chosen to serve the Prince of Peace and to bring God's blessing to all people. The Revelation to John is a warning: "Don't be foolish. The days may come when your trust in God will be tested. In fact, all the forces of hell and destruction may break loose against you. The story is not over yet."

All things new

The last two chapters end in a blaze of glory. The final act belongs to God. He will build his holy city, his new Jerusalem, for all the world to see. He will be with his people forever: "Behold, the dwelling of God is with men. He will dwell with them, and they shall be his people, and God himself will be with them; he will wipe away every tear from their eyes, and death shall be no more, neither shall there be mourning nor crying nor pain any more, for the former things have passed away."

Heaven on earth, complete with pearly gates and golden streets, is how John's vision pictures the end of the story. There is no need for a temple or for the sun or moon because the glory of God is present. Even the beauties of the Garden of Eden, complete with the tree of life, are there.

What would you want heaven to be like? Maybe a pure gold city as clear as glass is not your idea of heaven. Perhaps you would rather just have a place where you could live peacefully with your friends and forget about the jewels on the wall of the city. In any case, one day the God who created heaven and earth will complete his work of bringing his people back into relationship with him. Perhaps it will be in a garden paradise like Eden or in a heavenly city.

But God has not yet finished his work. The promise still remains: "And he who sat upon the throne said, 'Behold, I make all things new.' " Whether God and his Messiah will do all of this quickly or will continue to work slowly in the world through people, only God knows. We waste our time guessing. All we need to know is that he has chosen us and nothing can change that.

When the shadows of death or pain or sadness fall on our lives, we rest assured of God's final victory. There will be times as the stories of our lives unfold that we will remember the promise of our Lord, "Behold, I am coming soon." And when the story of God and his people seems as if it will never end, like those first Christians we may lift up our eyes and say, "Amen. Come, Lord Jesus!"

1. Revelation 1–3
2. Ezekiel 1, Daniel 7
3. Rev. 6:3-8
4. Revelation 5–8
5. Revelation 8–11
6. Revelation 12
7. Rev. 14:9-12

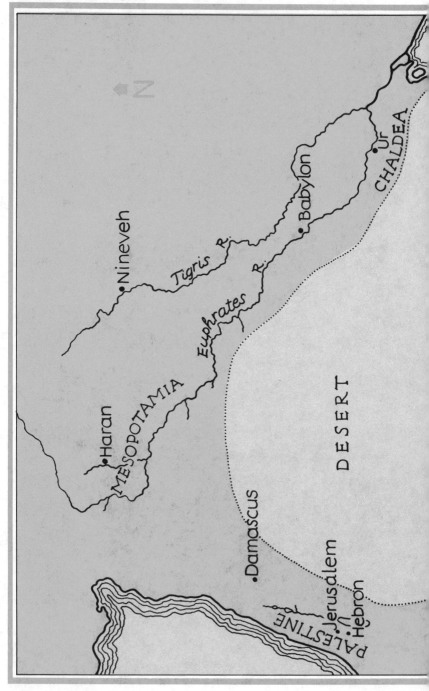

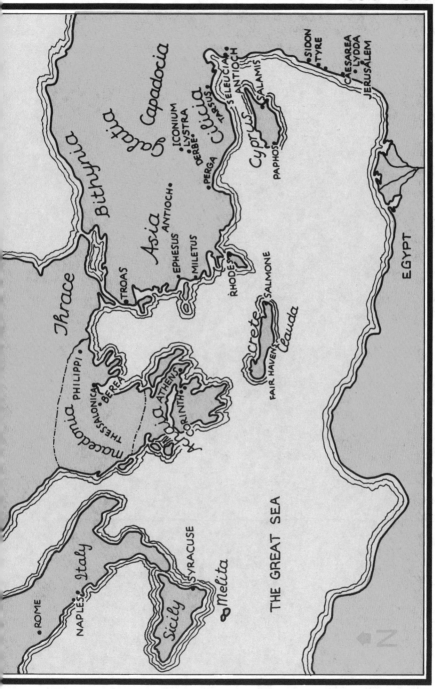